Dedication

To Troy, Landon and Tate

Acknowledgements

Special thanks to my grandparents and parents for passing down a spiritual heritage. And to Beth Corbitt, Troy Niles, Shelley Cline, Vickey Banks, Debby Faulkner, Phyllis Poe and Dr. Mark Hartman for their subsequent and distinctive roles in helping me achieve my dream.

Contents

Joy Of The Lord

~≈~

The happiness which brings enduring worth to life is not the superficial happiness that is dependent on circumstances. It is the happiness and content-ment that fills the soul even in the midst of the most distressing of circumstances and the most bitter environment....That kind of happiness stands in need of no outward stimulus.

~ Billy Graham

~≈~

To live happily is to live from within, relying on an inner power. To live happily is to live in the presence of God. And His presence comes by way of the Holy Spirit, our constant companion and Divine Guide Who offers glorious rewards and inspiration. Nehemiah 8:10 states: *The joy of the Lord is your strength.* The knowledge that His Spirit lives within us is the true secret of quiet, joyful strength. In affliction and trouble, our joy will know no bounds because we believe and trust in Him. We can live happily despite our circumstances, because His Spirit strengthens and satisfies our inner souls. Consider the inspiring words of St. Cyprian, written in the 3rd Century, shortly after his conversion to Christianity:

This is a cheerful world as I see it
from my garden under the shadows of my vines.
But if I were to ascend some high mountain
and look out over the wide lands,
you know very well what I should see:

brigands on the highways,
pirates on the sea,
armies fighting,
cities burning;
in the amphitheaters men murdered
to please applauding crowds;
selfishness and cruelty
and misery and despair
under all roofs.
It is a bad world, Donatus,
an incredibly bad world.
But I have discovered in the midst of it
a quiet and holy people
who have learned a great secret.
They have found a joy
which is a thousand times better
than any pleasure of our sinful life.
They are despised and persecuted,
but they care not.
They are masters of their souls.
They have overcome the world.
These people, Donatus, are the Christians —
and I am one of them.

Are you "one of them" about whom St. Cyprian wrote
— one who lives a quiet and holy life, who has mastered
the soul to overcome the world? Do you enjoy the rewards
of the inward power of the Holy Spirit, or are you still
struggling in the flesh and relying on your own strength?
If you are born of God, remember: *The one who is in you
is greater than the one who is in the world* (1 John 4:4).

~ Life Application ~

*I have told you this so that my joy may be in you
and that your joy may be complete.* John 15:11

1. The lives of the Thessalonians provide insight into the
    early Christians about whom Cyprian wrote. Read
    I Thessalonians Chapter 1. Let their quiet strength and
    desire for holiness inspire you to victoriously overcome
    the world. List the special qualities and characteristics of
    the church of the Thessalonians.

    _____

    _____

    _____

2. Read Galatians 2:20 and Romans 15:13. How should we live?

    _____

    _____

    _____

3. First John 5:4-5 states: *Everyone born of God overcomes the
    world. This is the victory that has overcome the world, even
    our faith. Who is it that overcomes the world? Only he who
    believes that Jesus is the Son of God.* What two ways do
    believers overcome the world?

    _____

    _____

    _____

~ Journal ~

The early Christians faced incredible persecution, yet they endured in their dedication and remained faithful to God's purposes. Likewise, with wholehearted obedience, we must strive to faithfully follow in their footsteps. Jesus once said, *"I have told you these things, so that in me you may have peace. In this world you will have trouble. But take heart! I have overcome the world"* (John 16:33). Ask God to fill you with His complete joy, to give you His strength to overcome the world.

_____

_____

_____

_____

_____

_____

_____

_____

_____

_____

_____

_____

_____

_____

_____

_____

Personal Journey

~~~

Our personal journeys mark us.
~ David Halberstam

~~~

Each of us must embark on a spiritual journey to discover who we are in God, for God has divine plans for our lives.

It is up to you to seek His guidance to find your unique purpose — to answer the question, "Why am I here?" The quality and success of your journey depends upon you. When you live your life only for yourself, never evaluating your purpose or seeking the will of God, your journey has no clear path or lasting gain; it is filled with darkness and hopelessness. But when you center your life on Christ, your travel brings meaning, and you experience a blessed journey, filled with hope, light, faith, joy, peace, and love.

If you will seek His divine wisdom you can travel the God-directed journey — a journey on which you will experience all the joy and beauty of a heart in tune with Christ.

Consider Pulitzer-prizewinning U.S. poet Robert Frost's poignant poem on fulfillment in life.

The Road Not Taken

Two roads diverged in a yellow wood,
  And sorry I could not travel both
And be one traveler, long I stood
  And looked down one as far as I could
To where it bent in the undergrowth;

Then took the other, as just as fair,
  And having perhaps the better claim,
Because it was grassy and wanted wear;
  Though as for that, the passing there
Had worn them really about the same,

And both that morning equally lay
  In leaves no step had trodden black.
Oh, I kept the first for another day!
  Yet knowing how way leads on to way,
I doubted if I should ever come back.

I shall be telling this with a sigh
  Somewhere ages and ages hence:
Two roads diverged in a wood, and I —
  I took the one less traveled by,
And that has made all the difference.[1]

Which road have you chosen? Have you chosen to live a God-directed journey? Recognizing God's sovereignty helps you fit into His master plan. Likewise, seeking the road less traveled — seeking to fulfill your higher purpose — will truly make all the difference in your life.

~ Life Application ~

I am the Lord your God, who teaches you what is best for you, who directs you in the way you should go. Isaiah 48:17

1. Isaiah 58:11 states: *The Lord will guide you always; he will satisfy your needs in a sun-scorched land and will strengthen your frame. You will be like a well-watered garden, like a spring whose waters never fail.* American preacher and political activist Henry Ward Beecher once said, "The strength and happiness of a man consists in finding out the way in which God is going, and in going that way too." Write out the prayer of Psalm 27:11. Ask God for His guidance and peace for your life.

   _____

   _____

   _____

2. What does Psalm 32:8 promise? What does verse 9 instruct?

   _____

   _____

3. Matthew 7:13-14 states: *Enter through the narrow gate. For wide is the gate and broad is the road that leads to destruction, and many enter through it. But small is the gate and narrow the road that leads to life, and only a few find it.* What do Proverbs 14:12 and Psalm 37:5-6 say?

   _____

   _____

~ Journal ~

No one comes to earth by accident. Each of us has a specific assignment — a purpose to fulfill while on our brief visit on earth. Why are you here? Have you discovered your purpose in life? Are you fulfilling it? Search your heart. As you answer these questions, ask God to help you seek the road less traveled.

_____

_____

_____

_____

_____

_____

_____

_____

_____

_____

_____

_____

_____

_____

_____

Eyes For The Eternal

~~~

To me, every hour of the day and night is an
unspeakably perfect miracle.
~ Walt Whitman (1819-1892)
American Poet

~~~

What a tragedy to simply exist in the ordinary, to be
content with the "mere act of seeing," living life blindly,
completely unaware of God's great beauty and blessings.
Think how different your life would be if you did treasure
each and every hour of your life and viewed it as a perfect
miracle. Helen Keller said it best:

> I have walked with people whose eyes are full of
> light but who see nothing in sea or sky, nothing in
> city streets, nothing in books. It were far better to
> sail forever in the night of blindness with sense,
> and feeling, and mind, than to be content with the
> mere act of seeing. The only lightless dark is the
> night of darkness in ignorance and insensibility.

We must not fail to be aware of our surroundings,
nor must we fail to look upon God in our world with
admiration and awe. Deuteronomy 4:9 tells us we must
strive to be in a state of awakening, learning,

understanding, and searching — a state of development, discovery, observation, expansion, comprehension, curiosity, reflection, and imagination.

Said M. Scott Peck:

> We have been looking for the burning bush, the parting of the sea, the bellowing voice from heaven. Instead we should be looking at the ordinary day-by-day events in our lives for evidences of the miraculous.

Strive to truly "see" the miracles in each and every hour of your life. Stay in a state of awareness, and learn to view each and every day as an endless possibility for miracles.

> *Be very careful never to forget what you have seen God doing for you. May His miracles have a deep and permanent effect upon your lives.*
>
> Deuteronomy 4:9 (TLB)

Make an effort to acknowledge God today; gratefully praise and thank Him for all He has done for you.

> *Many, O Lord my God,*
> *   are the wonders you have done.*
> *The things you planned for us*
> *   no one can recount to you;*
> *were I to speak and tell of them,*
> *   they would be too many to declare.*
>
> Psalm 40:5

~ Life Application ~

1. Second Corinthians 4:18 states: *We fix our eyes not on what is seen, but on what is unseen. For what is seen is temporary, but what is unseen is eternal.* Is your focus on the here and now? Are you only "seeing" the visible things? Write a prayer to God to help you see the unseen and the invisible —the miracles of Him.

    _____

    _____

    _____

2. What does Jesus promise in Luke 10:23-24 & John 20:29 to those who "see" into the mysteries of the kingdom?

    _____

    _____

3. What effect have His miracles and wonders had on you? Write about what you've personally seen Him do.

    _____

    _____

4. Finish these statements with evidence of His miracles.

    *   Thank you, God, for _____

    *   God, I recognize Your hand in _____

    *   God, I appreciate that You _____

    *   God, I see evidence of You in _____

~ Journal ~

We must not cease to wonder at the great marvels of our God. It would be very difficult to draw a line between holy wonder and real worship.

Charles Spurgeon

Do you regularly wonder at the great marvels of God? Are you content with the "mere act of seeing," living in a "lightless dark" of ignorance and insensibility to all that is around you? Find something of God's created beauty, or ponder a miracle which has had a deep and permanent effect on your life.

_____

_____

_____

_____

_____

_____

_____

_____

_____

_____

_____

_____

_____

Momentary Grace

~ ≈ ~

O momentary grace of mortal men, which we
hunt for more than the grace of God.
Hastings, *Richard the Third*
~ William Shakespeare

~ ≈ ~

In *Richard the Third*, shortly before his execution, Hastings realized his mistake of seeking the capricious graces of such self-seeking and powerful men as Richard and Edward IV. We often make the same mistake and search for favor and honor from the world — seeking our worth from riches, power, or knowledge.

We must fix our eyes on God and be ever mindful that the graces of the world are momentary, temporary and meaningless, but the grace of God is enduring and eternal.

St. Augustine of Hippo once wrote:
>Where your pleasure is, there your treasure:
>>Where your treasure,
>There your heart. Where your heart,
>>There your happiness.

The only way to find true happiness is to invest in the treasures of God. His spiritual treasures of knowledge, wisdom, and understanding promise to outlast any treasure you may obtain on earth. Silver and gold tarnish. Glory and honor fade. But, God's grace and love are everlasting. By placing your heart — your entire happiness and hope — in Christ Jesus and not in the temporal things of the world, you allow God to lift your soul and fill your heart with His eternal riches. Where are your treasure and your heart?

Pray the sincere prayer of Louisa May Alcott, American author of *Little Women*:

In Myself

I do not ask for any crown
But that which all may win;
Nor try to conquer any world
Except the one within.
Be thou my guide until I find
Led by a tender hand,
The happy kingdom in myself
And dare to take command!

Depend on and acknowledge Him in everything you do. Seek His grace first. Allow it to sustain and bless you.

Seek ye first the kingdom of God, and his righteousness; and all these things shall be added unto you.
Matthew 6:33 (KJV)

～ Life Application ～

We make a living by what we get, but we make a life by what we give....Remember that what you possess in the world will be found at the day of your death to belong to another, *but what you are will be yours forever.*

Henry van Dyke (1852-1933)
clergyman, Princeton professor, navy chaplain

1. Jesus said in Matthew 6:20-21 (KJV): *"Lay up for yourselves treasures in heaven...For where your treasure is, there will your heart be also."* What does Proverbs 24:3-4 say about treasures of the heart? How will you invest in these treasures?

    _____

    _____

    _____

    _____

2. Read Psalm 111:10 and Job 28:28. What do these verses mean?

    _____

    _____

    _____

3. What does 1 Timothy 6:17-19 say is uncertain? You should be rich in what?

    _____

    _____

    _____

~ Journal ~

They will lay up treasure for themselves as a firm foundation for the coming age, so that they may take hold of the life that is truly life.

1 Timothy 6:19

Are you seeking the enduring grace of God; or do you look for acceptance and worth from people and material possessions? How will you "lay up treasure" for yourself as a "firm foundation for the coming age"?

_____

_____

_____

_____

_____

_____

_____

_____

_____

_____

_____

_____

_____

_____

Growth Within

~≈~

The life which is unexamined is not worth living.

~ Plato (c. 427-347 B.C.)
Greek philosopher

~≈~

Michelangelo, artistic genius of the Renaissance, lived by his motto, "I am still learning." He sculpted the magnificient *David* while in his twenties, worked on the Sistene Chapel into his sixties, and worked on the rebuilding of St. Peter's Basilica well into his eighties.

Such should be our attitude. Our lives lose meaning when we are not growing and learning spiritually. God wants to teach us so much — to reveal "deep and hidden things." This revelation comes by way of self-examination and testing. It is His desire that we reflect on our past decisions, successes, and failures — that we question our motives and goals and the true attitude of our hearts, yet we are so busy looking all around us that we never look within. Treasures of wisdom, knowledge, and understanding await us; and Jesus is the key to them all. He is the pure light by which we can examine and test our hearts, for God made *His light shine in our hearts to give us the light of the knowledge of the glory of God* (2 Corinthians 4:6).

> Growth of man — like Growth of Nature —
> Gravitates within —
> Atmosphere, and Sun endorse it —
> But it stirs — alone —
>
> Each — its difficult Ideal
> Must achieve — Itself —
> Through the solitary prowess
> Of a Silent Life —
>
> ~ Emily Dickinson
> American poet (1830-1886)

Truly, growth gravitates within. Circumstances may help reveal it, but true growth occurs in the heart. Commit to improve, grow, and learn throughout your life.

Look into your heart and ascertain who you are in Christ — determine the true attitude of your heart.

> *He reveals deep and hidden things;*
> *he knows what lies in darkness,*
> *and light dwells with him.*
> Daniel 2:22

~ Life Application ~

1. Second Corinthians 13:5 states: *Examine yourselves to see whether you are in the faith; test yourselves. Do you not realize that Christ Jesus is in you — unless, of course, you fail the test?* Author Calvin Miller once said, "Character is who you are in the dark." Examine your heart right now. Are you genuine? Ask God to reveal deep and hidden things about yourself.

   _____

   _____

   _____

   _____

   _____

2. Read Psalm 44:21. What are the secrets of your heart?

   _____

   _____

   _____

   _____

   _____

3. Read Psalm 112:4-6. What will God do for the upright and righteous?

   _____

   _____

   _____

   _____

~ Journal ~

Let us examine our ways and test them. Lamentations 3:40

Do you regularly reflect on past decisions? Do you question your motives and goals? Is there true growth in your heart? What experience has God used, or is He using, to improve and grow you?

_____

_____

_____

_____

_____

_____

_____

_____

_____

_____

_____

_____

_____

_____

_____

_____

_____

_____

Life's Language

~∘~∘~

True love's the gift which God has given
   To man alone beneath the heaven;
It is the secret sympathy,
   The silver link, the silken tie,
Which heart to heart, and mind to mind,
   In body and in soul can bind.

from *Lay of the Last Minstrel*
~ Sir Walter Scott (1771-1832)
Scottish novelist, *Ivanhoe*

~∘~∘~

Love is life's most beautiful language. It is the message of God to the world, expressed through the gift of His son, Jesus Christ. When we truly listen to His message of love and allow it to penetrate every area of our hearts, it will provide complete fulfillment — a warmth and richness — to our lives that nothing else on earth can bring. Consider the famous 19th Century Dutch painter Vincent Van Gogh's word picture that illustrates his thoughts on love:

Love is something eternal — the aspect may change,
but not the essence.
There is the same difference in a person
before and after he is in love

as there is in an unlighted lamp
and one that is burning.
The lamp was there and it was a good lamp,
but now it is *shedding light*, too,
and that is its *real function*.

Surely, our real function in life is to shed the light of God. We were specifically created to share God's love — to speak His language of love to the world. To do this, we must allow the love of Jesus Christ to enter our hearts and completely fill our entire bodies — to fill every crack and crevice with His glorious light. Moreover, the more we come to truly know and completely rely on His great and perfect love, the more He will enable us to speak His language of love freely and unconditionally to others.

Fulfill your function of creation and let your lamp burn with the love of God. Freely and unconditionally share the language of God with others.

If I speak in the tongues of men and of angels
but have not love,
I am only a resounding gong
or a clanging cymbal.
1 Corinthians 13:1

∼ Life Application ∼

1. John 15:9-10 states: *As the Father has loved me, so have I loved you. Now remain in my love. If you obey my commands, you will remain in my love, just as I have obeyed my Father's commands and remain in his love.* How can you glorify Jesus the way He glorified the Father? What areas of your life need obedience?

   _____

   _____

   _____

   _____

2. What does Colossians 3:12-14 command?

   _____

   _____

   _____

   _____

3. Read Luke 11:33-36. Are you shedding light? Or are you the useless, unlighted lamp? How can you live to better exhibit the light?

   _____

   _____

   _____

   _____

~ Journal ~

You will find as you look back upon your life that
the moments that stand out, the moments when
you have really lived, are the moments when you
have done things in a spirit of love.

Henry Drummond

How will you share the spirit of love today? Determine who
in your world needs to hear the language of God. Then
determine how you will speak His language of love today.

_____

_____

_____

_____

_____

_____

_____

_____

_____

_____

_____

_____

_____

_____

_____

Sharpening The Ax

~∾~

If the ax is dull and its edge unsharpened, more strength is needed, but skill will bring success.

Ecclesiastes 10:10

~∾~

The 19th Century theologian John Henry Newman said it well: "Growth is the only evidence of life." We must strive to be constantly improving, growing, and developing in the Lord, lest we grow dull and unsharpened. Seeking His divine wisdom and understanding "sharpens our ax," thus quickening our knowledge of the things of God. If we ask for wisdom, He will give it to us. He will teach us good sense and restraint and give each of us a discerning, prudent, and understanding heart.

> Broad is the road that leads to death,
> And thousands walk together there;
> But wisdom shows a narrow path,
> With here and there a traveler.
>
> ~ Isaac Watts (1674-1748)
> English theologian and pastor,
> author of more than 500 hymns

Wisdom shows a narrow path. Seeking to gain this higher wisdom will teach the mystery of God, Himself, for if we accept, store up, turn, apply, call out, cry aloud, look, and search for the wisdom and understanding of God, then we will surely experience an inner victory and true enlightenment.

Commit yourself to traveling the narrow road. Search fervently for the wisdom of God.

> *My son, if you **accept** my words*
> > *and **store** up my commands within you,*
> *turning your ear to wisdom*
> > *and **applying** your heart to understanding,*
> *and if you **call out** for insight*
> > *and **cry aloud** for understanding,*
> *and if you **look** for it as for silver*
> > *and **search** for it as for hidden treasure,*
> *then you will **understand** the fear of the LORD*
> > *and **find** the knowledge of God,*
> *For the Lord gives wisdom,*
> > *And from his mouth come knowledge and*
> > > *understanding.*

Proverbs 2:1-6

∼ Life Application ∼

1. Proverbs 4:5-9 states: *Get wisdom, get understanding; do not forget my words or swerve from them. Do not forsake wisdom, and she will protect you; love her, and she will watch over you. Wisdom is supreme; therefore get wisdom. Though it cost all you have, get understanding. Esteem her, and she will exalt you; embrace her, and she will honor you.* Have you forsaken wisdom? How will you love, esteem, and embrace wisdom today?

   _____

   _____

2. Read James 1:5-8. What two things must we do to obtain wisdom?

   _____

3. Proverbs chapter 8 personifies wisdom as a woman calling to those who seek her. Verses 17-21 declare the promises of those who find her: *I love those who love me, and those who seek me find me. With me are riches and honor, enduring wealth and prosperity. My fruit is better than fine gold; what I yield surpasses choice silver. I walk in the way of righteousness, along the paths of justice, bestowing wealth on those who love me and making their treasuries full.* Read verses 32-36. What must we do for God to bestow His wealth on us and make our treasuries full?

   _____

~ Journal ~

*She (wisdom) will set a garland of grace on your head
and present you with a crown of splendor.* Proverb 4:9

Allow God to bestow a garland of grace and a crown of
splendor on your head. Begin by asking yourself the following
questions: Am I seeking the higher wisdom? Am I open to
instruction — learning, growing, and maturing in my
knowledge of God? Am I using the same, dull ax, or have I
allowed God to enhance and refine me? Ask God to sharpen
your ax and quicken your knowledge of Him.

_____

_____

_____

_____

_____

_____

_____

_____

_____

_____

_____

_____

_____

_____

_____

Living Water

~~~

God cannot give us happiness and peace apart
from Himself, because it is not there.
~ C. S. Lewis (1898-1963)
Christian author, apologist, Oxford professor

~~~

Jesus once said, *"Whoever believes in me… streams of living water will flow from within him"* (John 7:38). God's love is a sea of blessings — His waters are cool and pure, overflowing and abundant, refreshingly sweet to our souls. Moreover, His "living water" is able to meet our every need and satisfy our thirsty souls. But when we fail to live by the Spirit, we suffer great loss. Billy Sunday, the major league baseball player who became a great American evangelist, once said, "If you have no joy in your religion, there is a leak in your Christianity." That leak is our lack of reliance on the power of the Holy Spirit, the "living water" that flows springs of love, joy, and peace in our hearts. Without His fellowship, we are drained of inner peace. As David described, *"My moisture is turned into the drought of summer"* (Psalm 32:4 KJV). The fruit of the spirit literally dissolves from our life. Our faith becomes barren, and our joy becomes dry and parched — our hearts become as a bountiless wasteland. Truly, fullness of joy is found only in the presence of God (Psalm 16:11).

Nineteenth Century British poet Christina Rossetti wrote a beautiful poem on seeking this "living water."

Lord, we are rivers running to thy sea,
Our waves and ripples all derived from Thee:
A nothing we should have, a nothing be,
Except for thee.
Sweet are the waters of thy shoreless sea,
Make sweet our waters that make haste to thee;
Pour in thy sweetness, that ourselves may be
Sweetness to thee.

When your "moisture" is gone, seek out the "living water" of God. Allow His sweet Spirit to overflow blessings, to provide you with abundant life, flourishing with His fruits — fruits of love, joy, peace, patience, kindness, goodness, and faithfulness.

To him who is thirsty I will give to drink without cost from the spring of the water of life.
                                        Revelation 21:6

~ Life Application ~

1. Jeremiah 31:12 states: *They will come and shout for joy on the heights of Zion; they will rejoice in the bounty of the Lord — the grain, the new wine and the oil, the young of the flocks and herds. They will be like a well-watered garden, and they will sorrow no more.* God promises to fill His people with bounty. Are you filled with the bounty of the Lord? Read John 14:16-18 and put these verses in your own words.

    _____

    _____

    _____

    _____

    _____

2. What does John 10:10 promise?

    _____

    _____

    _____

3. Read John 4:3-14. Ask God to fill you with His "living water" to urge and prompt you to live a righteous life.

    _____

    _____

    _____

    _____

~ Journal ~

The fruit of the Spirit is love, joy, peace, patience, kindness, goodness, faithfulness, gentleness and self-control. Galatians 5:22-23

Is a specific fruit lacking in your life? If so, petition the Spirit of God to change your heart and fill you with the fruit of His love.

_____

_____

_____

_____

_____

_____

_____

_____

_____

_____

_____

_____

_____

_____

_____

_____

I Can Do All Things

~∾~

One can never consent to creep when one feels
an impulse to soar.

~ Helen Keller

~∾~

Helen Keller was truly one of the most remarkable people to ever walk the earth. Mark Twain said of her: "She will be as famous a thousand years from now as she is today." Helen's words and life inspire us to endeavor to live better lives. Despite being blind, deaf, and mute from early childhood, Helen led a fulfilled life in a society that had little or no use for the handicapped, believing them fit only for insane asylums. Yet, Helen never let others' low expectations limit her, nor did she yield to self-pity and fear. She achieved far beyond the average sighted and hearing person. Helen wrote books, rode horseback, acted in movies, graduated Magna Cum Laude from Radcliffe College, and served in the war effort. She lectured publicly all over the United States after learning to speak by touching the mouth and vocal chords of her teacher, Annie Sullivan. But most of all, she changed hundreds of thousands of lives through her work for the handicapped.

Helen wrote these profound words:

"It is difficult for me to answer when I am asked what are the main lessons life has taught me....I found my greatest satisfaction in working with men and women everywhere who ask not, 'Shall I labor among Christians or Jews or Buddhists?' but say rather, 'God, in thy wisdom help me to decrease the sorrows of thy children and increase their advantages and joys.' Blindness and deafness were simply the banks that guided the course of my life-ship until the stream joined the sea....

"I discovered in my Greek sayings, 'There is no force so mighty in the world as perseverence.'...

"Varied thoughts convince me that, blind or seeing, one is not happy unless one's heart is filled with the sun which never dissolves into gloom. God is that sun, and if one's faith in Him is only strong, He will somehow or other reveal one's powers and brighten the darkest days with His divine beams."

Let Helen's life-example inspire you to persevere. Let God be your sun, and allow your faith in Him to guide the course of your life-ship, to encourage you to press on toward creative accomplishment.

To those who by persistence in doing good seek glory, honor and immortality, he will give eternal life.
                                                    Romans 2:7

~ Life Application ~

Philippians 4:13 (KJV) states: *I can do all things through Christ which strengtheneth me.* We, like Helen, can achieve the incredible and accomplish anything when we put our trust in Christ and allow His power to fill our souls.

1. First Corinthians 16:13-14 states: *Be on your guard; stand firm in the faith; be men of courage; be strong. Do everything in love.* What does Hebrews 10:23-24 tell you?

    _____

    _____

    _____

    _____

2. Helen Keller certainly knew about determination and perseverance. What does Hebrews 10:35-38 say about perseverance and faith?

    _____

    _____

    _____

    _____

3. Hebrews 3:5-6 urges us to hold on to what?

    _____

    _____

    _____

    _____

～ Journal ～

How are you using your "banks" — your handicaps — to decrease the sorrows of others and increase their advantages and joys? Contemplate the course of your life-ship. What oceans will you sail? How will you sail them to make a difference in the world?

_____

_____

_____

_____

_____

_____

_____

_____

_____

_____

_____

_____

_____

_____

_____

_____

_____

_____

Felt With The Heart

~≈~

The best and most beautiful things in the world cannot be seen or even touched. They must be felt with the heart.

~ Helen Keller

~≈~

When Annie Sullivan spelled "I love Helen," into her hand, Helen was perplexed by the word "love." At that time, she comprehended very few words, and all those words were concrete — the things she could physically touch. In simpler words, Annie explained "love" to Helen like this:

Love is something like the clouds that were in the sky before the sun came out....You cannot touch the clouds, you know; but you feel the rain and know how glad the flowers and the thirsty earth are to have it after a hot day. You cannot touch love either; but you feel the sweetness that it pours into everything. Without it you would not be happy or want to play

Helen understood.

The beautiful truth burst upon my mind. I felt that these were invisible lines stretched between my spirit and the spirit of others.

Love is the language that speaks directly to the heart. It also connects us spiritually to each other. Yet, only the pure and perfect love of Christ can enable us to truly understand and act on a love beyond all human comprehension and reasoning, for when we live in His love, we become privy to the best and most beautiful Love in the world.

Envision the invisible lines of love that connect you to God and others, and feel its incomparable force.

The Heart of Love

April cold with dropping rain
Willows and lilacs bring again,
The whistle of returning birds,
And the trumpet — lowing of the herds.
The scarlet maple — keys betray
What potent blood hath modest May,
What fiery force the earth renews,
The wealth of forms, the flush of hues;
What joy in rosy waves outpoured
Flows from the heart of love, the Lord.

~ Ralph Waldo Emmerson (1803-1882)
American poet

Allow the joy of the Lord to flow from His heart to yours. Let His love engulf you, then share it with those around you.

~ Life Application ~

God is love. Whoever lives in love
lives in God,
and God in him.
1 John 4:16

1. What does 1 John 4:7-8 mean to you?

    _____

    _____

    _____

    _____

2. Matthew 22:37-39(KJV) states: *Thou shalt love the Lord*
    thy God with all thy heart, and with all thy soul, and with all
    thy mind. This is the first and greatest commandment. And
    the second is like unto it, Thou shalt love thy neighbor as
    thyself. Read 1 John 3:18. How can you best pour out your
    love on others "with all actions and in truth"? Be specific.

    _____

    _____

    _____

    _____

3. Read 1 Peter 1:22. How should we love each other?

    _____

    _____

    _____

~ Journal ~

Love connects us spiritually to each other. What does love mean to you? To whom are you spiritually connected? How can you act upon the love you feel?

_____

_____

_____

_____

_____

_____

_____

_____

_____

_____

_____

_____

_____

_____

_____

_____

_____

_____

_____

Lost And Found

~≈~

It fortifies my soul to know
That, though I perish,
Truth is so:
That, howsoe'er I stray
And range,
Whate'er I do, Thou dost
not change
I steadier step when I recall
That, if I slip, *Thou dost
not fall*.
~ Arthur Hugh Clough
English poet (1819-1861)

~≈~

Like the prodigal son in the Bible, we sometimes turn our backs on God's instruction and turn our hearts away from His will in pursuit of our own wants and desires. In our selfishness, we stray far from God, only to find ourselves in a "distant country," tired and weary, and in desperate need. What a comfort to know that we can always return home. God's mercy knows no bounds! His love is unconditional — it remains the same, despite our actions. When we go to Him in true repentance, and cast ourselves humbly on His mercy, He will run and meet us, and will lovingly receive us with open arms. He will shower us with His rich grace and restore our fellowship with Him.

Christian author Max Lucado once said, "We think God's love rises and falls with our performance. It doesn't….He loves you for whose you are: You are His child." God's mercy endures forever. "His truth is so." No matter what we do, God will not change. He remains right there, quietly waiting, ready to run and meet us and freely forgive us. Truly, our walk with God becomes stronger when we rely on and trust in His grace and mercy — when we draw near to Him with a sincere heart in full assurance of faith (Hebrews 10:22).

Take great comfort in God's tenderness — in His willingness to forgive, and forgive, and forgive. Don't be afraid to return to Him to receive His wonderful gift of grace, for *His love will welcome you*. It *will clothe you in the best of robes*; it will *place shoes on your feet* and *bestow a ring on your hand. His love will rejoice over you.*

> *Let me fall into the hands of the Lord for his mercy is very great.*
> 1 Chronicles 21:13

~ Life Application ~

1. Read the Parable of the Prodigal son (Luke 15:11-32) and experience the mercy of God. What does this parable mean to you? What special actions of the father mean the most to you? Why?

   _____

   _____

   _____

   _____

2. Hebrews 10:22 states: *Let us draw near to God with a sincere heart in full assurance of faith, having our hearts sprinkled to cleanse us from a guilty conscience and having our bodies washed with pure water.* What does Psalm 103:12 state about sin? What is the promise of John 6:37?

   _____

   _____

   _____

   _____

3. What does Daniel 9:9 state? Micah 7:18-19 states that God will fulfill what promise?

   _____

   _____

   _____

   _____

~ Journal ~

Draw near to God with a sincere heart. Write a prayer of thanksgiving to Him for removing your sins as far as the east is from the west, and for the gracious gift of His son, which made forgiveness possible.

_____

_____

_____

_____

_____

_____

_____

_____

_____

_____

_____

_____

_____

_____

_____

_____

_____

_____

Iron Sharpens Iron

~∼~

The person who tries to live alone will not succeed
as a human being. His heart withers if it does not
answer another heart. His mind shrinks away if he
hears only the echoes of his own thought and no
other inspirations.

~ Pearl S. Buck (1892-1973)
Nobel-prizewinning American author

~∼~

God uses the people in our lives, especially those
closest to us, to communicate to us and teach us — to
show us truths about life, ourselves, and even Himself.
Each one of our lives is like an enormously complex
puzzle, created by circumstances, experiences, and people
— people who have been indefinitely placed by God,
and people who, for some specific purpose, stay only for
a brief time. We are a puzzle that is as yet unfinished.
Each of us still has lessons to learn and love to share —
to consequently fill in the missing pieces and to help
complete the lives of others. When our hearts are open
and willing to share and learn from those around us, God
will teach us great lessons. Moreover, He will use our

friends, co-workers, spouses, parents and children as tools to improve our character flaws and weaknesses; tools to strengthen our talents and abilities; tools to comfort us and soothe the pain of our suffering and to encourage us and show His love to us.

> I sought my soul,
> But my soul I could not see.
> I sought my God,
> But my God eluded me.
> I sought my brother,
> And I found all three.
> ~ Anonymous

Be open and willing to learn and answer the hearts of those who enter your realm of life. Listen. Learn. And above all, allow God to subsist in the heart of your life's lessons.

As iron sharpens iron, so one man sharpens another.
Proverbs 27:17

~ Life Application ~

There are two ways of spreading light:
to be the candle
or the mirror that receives it.

~ Edith Wharton (1862-1937)
American novelist and poet

Most certainly, one person can sharpen the life of another if that "life" is open and willing to learn. Are you truly willing to learn from the people in your life? Consider why God brought them into the realm of your existence. Consider His timing. Be assured that He has a specific and definite purpose in mind for each. Now, contemplate the "pieces" to the puzzle of your life. What have you learned, or are you in the process of learning, from them, and they from you? What expressly has their life offered to you?

A. Parents _____

B. Spouse _____

C. Brothers/Sisters _____

D. Children _____

E. Friends _____

F. Co-workers_____

G. Role models (i.e. pastors, teachers, leaders) ____

H. Grandparents/other relatives _____

I. Others of significance _____

~ Journal ~

How will you spread the light of encouragement and inspiration — the light of truth and goodness to others? To whom specifically will you reflect it? How will you receive light? Whose life will you mirror and be inspired by? Who do you believe arrived in your life's realm for a very clear and definite purpose?

_____

_____

_____

_____

_____

_____

_____

_____

_____

_____

_____

_____

_____

_____

_____

_____

_____

_____

Point Of Time

~∽~

The whole life of man is but a point of time;
let us enjoy it, therefore, while it lasts, and
not spend it to no purpose.

~ Plutrarch (c. A.D. 46-120)
Greek philosopher and biographer

~∽~

Life is good. We should revel and rejoice in every precious day. Our point of time should be lived to the fullest, but always with perspective and purpose. Perspective reminds us that life is simply too short to be wasted on meaningless details. Purpose reminds us to compare the brevity of our lives with eternity — to keep focusing on our final reward. Hence, Alan Watts' profound words on living a fuller life:

> No one imagines that a symphony is supposed to improve in quality as it goes along, or that the whole object of playing it is to reach the finale. The point of music is discovered in every moment of playing and listening to it. It is the same, I feel, with the greater part of our lives, and if we are unduly absorbed in improving them we may forget altogether to live them.

We cannot become overly absorbed in the details of each day, nor should we get caught up in improving our tomorrows. Instead, we must live each day with perspective and purpose. Our focus must be on fulfilling our assignment from God and enjoying each and every day to its fullest.

Remember that life on earth and all it entails is temporary; moreover, it is meaningless when God is not your primary focus. Celebrate and delight in God's abundant goodness. Keep laughing, appreciating, and enjoying life while pursuing, serving, and worshipping God.

> *Light is sweet,*
> *and it pleases the eyes to see the sun.*
> *However many years a man may live,*
> *let him enjoy them all.*
> *But let him remember the days of darkness,*
> *for they will be many.*
> *Everything to come is meaningless.*
> Ecclesiastes 11:7-8

~ Life Application ~

1. Psalm 39:5 states: *You have made my days a mere handbreadth; the span of my years is as nothing before you. Each man's life is but a breath.* Read 1 Corinthians 7:29-31. What is Paul's advice on how to live?

   _____

   _____

   _____

   _____

   _____

2. Read Job 8:8-20. What is the destiny of all those who forget God?

   _____

   _____

   _____

   _____

3. Read Psalm 62:9-12. What does the psalmist say about life on earth? What truly matters in the end?

   _____

   _____

   _____

   _____

   _____

~ Journal ~

The point of life, like the point of music, is in the process. Have you found the point to your life? Have you learned to enjoy your point of time? How do you intend to best fulfill your purpose, to complete your special assignment from God?

_____

_____

_____

_____

_____

_____

_____

_____

_____

_____

_____

_____

_____

_____

_____

_____

_____

_____

_____

Growing In Grace

~~~

Being a Christian is more than just an instantaneous conversion — it is a daily process whereby you grow to be more and more like Christ.

~ Billy Graham (1918-)
U.S. Evangelist

~~~

True Christianity begins in the heart, continues in patience, and endures to seek the glory and honor of God — to seek the final promise of Christianity — immortality. It involves true worship that has very little to do with religion and its traditions; instead, it has everything to do with dying to self and abounding in Christ —growing in grace and in the knowledge of the Lord (2 Peter 3:18). The person who is truly growing to be more and more like Christ is the person who daily follows the example of Christ. It is the person who constantly and sincerely seeks righteousness and honors and reverences Christ with all his heart.

An important part of the "daily process" of growing to be more like Christ involves dying to self. The more

Christ increases within us, the more we (our fleshly nature) will decrease. Paul explained it like this: *"I have been crucified with Christ and I no longer live, but Christ lives in me."* And: *"In the same way, count yourselves dead to sin but alive to God in Christ Jesus...for sin shall not be your master, because you are not under law, but under grace"* (Galatians 2:20; Romans 6:11, 14).

In the following prayer, the 15th Century Dutch theologian and scholar, Desiderius Erasmus, wrote about his desire to grow in Christ:

> Sever me from myself that I may be grateful to you;
> May I perish to myself that I may be safe in you;
> May I die to myself that I may live in you;
> May I wither to myself that I may blossom in you;
> May I be emptied of myself that I may abound in you;
> May I be nothing to myself that I may be all in you.

Go before God with a willing and humble attitude. Surrender your soul to His will, so you glorify Him in all you do.

We are made partakers of Christ, if we hold the beginning of our confidence steadfast unto the end.
                                                    Hebrews 3:14 (KJV)

~ Life Application ~

1. Isaiah 29:13 states: *These people come near to me with their mouth and honor me with their lips. Their worship of me is made up only of rules taught by men.* True Christianity involves the heart, not rules and traditions. Is your worship truly from the heart, or are you simply practicing the rules and traditions of religion — going through the motions of Christianity? What does James 4:8 say you should do?

   _____

   _____

   _____

2. First Corinthians 3:1-3 states: *Brothers, I could not address you as spiritual but as worldly — mere infants in Christ. I gave you milk, not solid food, for you were not yet ready....You are still worldly.* Are you still worldly, a spiritual infant surviving only on milk? Contemplate your spiritual maturity. Ask God to help you grow in grace and in the knowledge of Him.

   _____

   _____

   _____

3. Hebrews 3:14 instructs the believer to hold steadfastly to Christ unto the end. What does Philippians 3:12-16 direct you to do?

   _____

   _____

~ Journal ~

Contemplate your heart attitude. Have you died to self? Are you truly abounding in the Lord and growing in His grace? Sincerely pray Erasmus' prayer. Humbly, write out your own prayer of submission and consecration to the Lord.

_____

_____

_____

_____

_____

_____

_____

_____

_____

_____

_____

_____

_____

_____

_____

_____

_____

_____

_____

_____

Sufficient Grace

~~~

Life's difficult. This is a great truth, one of the greatest truths. It is a great truth because once we truly see this truth, we transcend it. Once we truly know that life is difficult — once we truly understand and accept it — then life is no longer difficult. Because once it is accepted, the fact that life is difficult no longer matters.

~ M. Scott Peck

~~~

Acceptance makes life easier. Once we learn to patiently accept what can't be changed and courageously work to change what needs to be changed, life will take on new meaning. Paul's life example transcended this very truth. During beatings, stonings, imprisonment, and the continual threat of death, he sang and praised God. He overflowed with joy and gratitude. For him, life was difficult, yet, it didn't matter because he firmly believed God's grace to be sufficient. Amazingly, he delighted *in weaknesses, in insults, in hardships, in persecutions, in difficulties* because they made him grow stronger (2 Corinthians 12:10).

The Scottish historian and philosopher Thomas

Carlyle once said, "The tragedy of life is not so much what men suffer, but rather what they miss." In our pain and sorrow, we too often miss the blessings and provisions of God. Sadly, we take no notice of His faithfulness — His promise to never leave us nor forsake us. We also overlook His compassion — His overwhelming, unconditional mercy and love that provides comfort to us in all our troubles. Moreover, we pay no regard to His sovereignty —His omnipotent power and His ability to make all things possible. We cannot let our sufferings allow us to miss the qualities of God's character — a character that is holy, gentle, forgiving, gracious, perfect, patient, mighty, unique, and understanding.

Yet, in the maddening maze of things,
and tossed by storm and flood,
to one fixed trust my spirit clings:
I know that God is good!

~~~

I have no answer, for myself or thee,
Save that I learned beside my mother's knee:
All is of God that is, and is to be;
And God is good. Let this suffice us still,
Resting in childlike trust upon his will
Who moves to his great ends unthwarted by the ill.

~ John Greenleaf Whittier (1807-1892)
Quaker poet, abolitionist, author of many hymns

~ Life Application ~

My grace is sufficient for you. 2 Corinthians 12:9

1. Romans 8:28 states: *We know that in all things God works for the good of those who love him, who have been called according to his purpose.* Read Jeremiah 29:11. How do we know that God will work everything out for the good to fit His ultimate plan?

    _____

    _____

    _____

2. Shakespeare once wrote, "There's a divinity that shapes our ends, Rough hew them how we will." Ultimately, God is in control of your life. But, you do have control of one aspect, and that is your attitude, the way you respond to life's circumstances. What does Philippians 4:6 say your reaction to life should be?

    _____

    _____

    _____

3. We must completely trust God, especially in trials and struggles. Read 2 Corinthians 6:3-10. What do these verses say to you personally?

    _____

    _____

    _____

~ Journal ~

O God, give us the serenity to accept what cannot be changed; the courage to change what should be changed; and wisdom to distinguish one from the other.

~ Reinhold Niebuhr (1892-1971)
Protestant Theologian

Write your own prayer of acceptance and faith to the Lord.

_____

_____

_____

_____

_____

_____

_____

_____

_____

_____

_____

_____

_____

_____

_____

_____

_____

In The Shadow Of The Almighty

~∾~

I know the Bible is inspired because it inspires me.
~ D. L. Moody (1837-1899)
American evangelist and missionary

~∾~

Corrie ten Boom told an incredible, true story of a prisoner in a concentration camp.

One day while reading the promises of Psalm 91 — *He who dwells in the shelter of the Most High will rest in the shadow of the Almighty* — this prisoner prayed aloud to God, "God I want to live and serve you, but everyone is dying around me. Let me live!" He then heard an inner voice that replied to him, "Rely on what you heard, and go home." He immediately obeyed by packing his things and walking toward the gates. He was stopped by the guards, and he simply told them, "I am under the protection of the Most High." Remarkably, he wasn't shot; moreover, he was allowed to pass through two more gates without incident. Because this prisoner listened to God and was courageously obedient to His voice, he escaped that day to be the only survivor of that entire concentration camp. Incidentally, Hitler was known throughout the German army by the title, "Most High."

This prisoner's incredible story reminds us not only to read God's Word, but to act on it. Joseph Cook once said, "Do you know a book that you are willing to put under your head for a pillow when you lie dying? That is the book you want to study while you are living. There is but one such book in the world. The Bible." The Word of God is a treasure chest filled with unsurpassed riches. Gems of wisdom and insight are available to guide you on your journey. Jewels of peace, hope and joy await your discovery. Everything you could possibly desire to enrich and fulfill your soul can be found in His Word. Today, fervently search the Bible to find His promises for you. Listen carefully to His words, and let them inspire your life's journey.

We search the world for truth;
We cull the good, the pure, the beautiful,
From all old flower fields of the soul;
And, weary seekers of the best,
We come back laden from our quest,
To find that all the sages said
Is in the Book our mothers read.
~ Whittier

Thy word is a lamp unto my feet, and a light unto my path.
Psalm 119:105 (KJV)

~ Life Application ~

1.   Truly, the Bible has the power to penetrate our innermost being. No other book is as powerful: *The word of God is living and active. Sharper than any double-edged sword, it penetrates even to dividing soul and spirit, joints and marrow; it judges the thoughts and attitudes of the heart* (Hebrews 4:12). Read Psalm 19:7-11 and Joshua 1:8. How will God's Word affect your life?

   _____

   _____

   _____

2.   It is foolish to live without guidance from God. The Bible provides all the answers to life. *The whole Bible was given to us by inspiration from God and is useful to teach us what is true and to make us realize what is wrong in our lives; it straightens us out and helps us do what is right* (2 Timothy 3:16 TLB). Do you regularly spend time in God's Book? What do Deuteronomy 29:29 and Romans 10:17 say about God's Word?

   _____

   _____

   _____

3.   What do Matthew 24:35 and Psalm 119:89-96 say?

   _____

   _____

   _____

~ Journal ~

The words of the Lord are flawless, like silver refined in a furnace of clay, purified seven times. Psalm 12:6

God's word is perfect. Find a treasure of insight for your life — a favorite verse or one that speaks directly to you in your situation. Write it in your journal; then, listen and react to His voice. Believe in it, and let it light your path — it will not return void. (Isaiah 55:11)

_____

_____

_____

_____

_____

_____

_____

_____

_____

_____

_____

_____

_____

_____

_____

_____

Promises Of Resurrection

~∾~

Our Lord has written the promises of the resurrection, not in books alone, but in every leaf in springtime.

~ Martin Luther (1483-1546)
German theologian, preacher, religious reformer

~∾~

God's promises are evident in the intricacies of life. We see rebirth and rejuvenation in all creatures and elements of nature — every new leaf, each blossoming bud and blade of grass with the onset of spring. Most confirming for our position of faith is the process of the formation of life, for who cannot see evidence of God when he looks upon the tiny face, hands, and feet of a newborn infant!

Isaiah 11:9 states: *The earth will be full of the knowledge of the Lord as the waters cover the sea.* Clearly, the God of all nature specifically designed the world to fully glorify Himself and reflect His magnificence and majesty. He left the fingerprints of His eternal power and divine nature — fingerprints that provide us with the blessed assurance of the miracle of the third day. Hence, the beautiful prayer of Christina Rossetti:

Lord, grant us eyes to see
Within the seed a tree,
Within the glowing egg a bird,
Within the shroud a butterfly:
Till taught by such, we see
Beyond all creatures thee,
And hearken for thy tender word
And hear it, "Fear not: it is I."

Search for God's promise of the resurrection in all creation. Rejoice in the miracle of the third day — the miracle that ensures the promise of eternal life.

The heavens declare the glory of God;
The skies proclaim the work of his hands.
Day after day they pour forth speech;
night after night they display knowledge.

There is no speech or language
where their voice is not heard.
Their voice goes out into all the earth,
Their words to the ends of the world.

Psalm 19:1-4

~ Life Application ~

1. Romans 1:20 states: *Since the creation of the world God's invisible qualities — his eternal power and divine nature — have been clearly seen, being understood from what has been made.* In Psalm 36:5-9 how is nature similar to the Creator's benevolence and greatness?

   _____

   _____

   _____

   _____

2. Read Jeremiah 10:12-13. What do the earth and the sky reflect?

   _____

   _____

   _____

3. Colossians 1:16-17 states: *By him all things were created: things in heaven and on earth, visible and invisible, whether thrones or powers or rulers or authorities; all things were created by him and for him. He is before all things, and in him all things hold together.* Jesus is, literally, the image of the invisible God. He was before the created world, and He is all eternity. Jesus holds together all creation. What does 1 Corinthians 15:20-23 say about His resurrection?

   _____

   _____

   _____

~ Journal ~

Often, people who visit the Grand Canyon, Niagara Falls, the mountains, or the ocean for the first time cannot escape the overwhelming greatness and awesomeness of God. Think of a time when God's divine glory was revealed to you through nature. Record your experience with the Creator of the universe.

_____

_____

_____

_____

_____

_____

_____

_____

_____

_____

_____

_____

_____

_____

_____

_____

_____

_____

_____

Everlasting Life

~~~

It is a far, far better thing that I do, than I have ever
done; it is a far, far better rest that I go to, than I
have ever known.

<div style="text-align: right">

Sidney Carton's final words in *A Tale of Two Cities*
~ Charles Dickens
English novelist

</div>

~~~

In *A Tale of Two Cities* Sidney Carton was transformed
from a depressed and hopeless alcoholic to a man who
demonstrated the ultimate act of sacrifice — dying for a
friend. What could have inspired such an incredible
transformation? Sidney's metamorphosis began with the
words read at his father's grave:

I am the resurrection and the life, saith the Lord;
he that believeth in me, though he were dead, yet
shall he live: and whosoever liveth and believeth in
me, shall never die.[2]

These profound words sparked a glimmer of hope
within Sidney and compelled him to embark on a journey
to answer some of life's most universal questions,
questions concerning purpose, God, and eternity. His
search eventually landed him directly at the foot of the
cross. Years of bitterness, despair, and hopelessness

disappeared in a repentant prayer for mercy. The realm of possibility and conceivability unearthed, the Truth was at last realized. Indeed, Sidney found that all of the answers to his search for life's true meaning and purpose rested in Christ's death on the cross. And with the cross, came the realization of the blessed hope — the assurance that because of His sacrifice, death in this life is but the beginning of everlasting peace and love.

The enormity of Christ's love humbled and over-whelmed Sidney. His heart was completely transformed by the love of Christ, a love that satisfied his spirit and inspired him to make the ultimate sacrifice. It was Christ's love that strengthened him and enabled him to peacefully wait his turn at the guillotine. It was His love that helped him encourage and comfort another also in line — a woman who said to Sidney just before her execution:

> "But for you, dear stranger, I should not be so composed…nor should I have been able to raise my thoughts to Him who was put to death, that we might have hope and comfort here today. I think you were sent to me by Heaven."[3]

For God so loved the world, that he gave his only begotten Son, that whosoever believeth in him should not perish, but have everlasting life.

John 3:16 KJV

~ Life Application ~

1. Contemplate the words of Gerard Manley Hopkins, 17th
    Century Jesuit priest and English poet:
    > Thou, thou, my Jesus, after me
    > Didst reach thine arms out of dying,
    > For my sake sufferedst nails and lance,
    > Mocked and marred countenance,
    > Sorrows passing number,
    > Sweat and care and cumber,
    > Yea and death, and this for me.

    They echo the prophetic words of Isaiah 53. Read Isaiah
    53. Reflect on Jesus' immense suffering and sacrifice, a
    sacrifice that He made especially for you. Contemplate
    the enormity of his overwhelming love. Then, write out
    verse 5, placing your name where applicable.

    _____

    _____

2. Read Mark 15:16-38, the actual account of Jesus' death.

3. St. Augustine once said, "He loves each one of us, as if
    there were only one of us." First John 3:1 states: *Behold,
    what manner of love the Father hath bestowed upon us, that
    we should be called the sons of God* (KJV). Record your
    gratitude and thanks to God for bestowing His love on
    you with His selfless sacrifice.

    _____

    _____

~ Journal ~

Jesus has promised, *"All that the Father giveth me shall come to me; and him that cometh to me I will in no wise cast out"* (John 6:37 KJV). We have the assurance of a God who deeply desires our fellowship — a God who promises to complete the good work, which He began in us. Nourish your relationship with Him. Allow Him to meet your deepest needs. Prayerfully search for God with all your heart — seek His will for your life. Then share your soul with Him.

_____

_____

_____

_____

_____

_____

_____

_____

_____

_____

_____

_____

_____

_____

_____

_____

_____

Whom Shall I Fear?

~〜~

Far better it is to dare mighty things, to win glorious
triumphs, even though checkered by failure, than
to rank with those poor spirits who neither enjoy
much nor suffer much, because they live in the gray
twilight that know not victory or defeat.

~ Theodore Roosevelt
26th U.S. President

~〜~

The great American inventor Thomas Edison, who
had over 1,000 patents issued in his name, once said,
"Show me a thoroughly satisfied man, and I will show
you a failure." Incredibly, before Edison found the best
material to use as filament for his light bulb, he tried
thousands of other materials! He won glorious triumphs
in his life because he never let failure stop him from daring
mighty things — he simply overcame failure with faith.
Edison went on to say, "I never did anything in life worth
doing by accident, nor did any of my inventions come
by accident." Such is the essence of our faith, for faith
does not happen by accident — it is a perpetual exercise
— a daily application of God's promises. Moreover, we

accomplish much and win mighty victories by way of our faith. When we continuously work to strengthen our faith day after day, we learn to persevere in taking on the obstacles of life to eventually replace all our fear with faithfulness. Hence, Fanny Crosby's hymn on the victory of faith:

Conquering now and still to conquer,
Rideth a King in His might;
Leading the host of all the faithful
into the midst of the fight;
See them with courage advancing,
clad in their brilliant array,
Shouting the name of their Leader,
hear them exultantly say:
Not to the strong is the battle,
Not to the swift is the race,
Yet to the true and the faithful
Victory is promised through grace.

Don't live in the gray twilight that doesn't know victory or defeat. Replace all your fear with faithfulness. Be ever faithful to dare — to learn from your past mistakes and to discover your hidden talents. Allow failure to teach you and grow you — to motivate you to persevere and receive the victory promised through grace.

Remember the words of Alfred, Lord Tennyson:
"If you fear cast all your cares on God; that anchor holds."

~ Life Application ~

The Lord is my light and my salvation;
Whom shall I fear?
The Lord is the defense of my life;
Whom shall I dread?
Psalm 27:1 (NAS)

1. Isaiah 41:13 states: *I am the Lord, your God, who takes hold of your right hand and says to you, Do not fear; I will help you.* What does Psalm 55:22 say?

    _____

    _____

    _____

    _____

2. What do Romans 8:15 and 1 John 4:18 say about fear? Using these verses, write a one-sentence prayer to God, asking for His strength and courage to overcome your fear.

    _____

    _____

    _____

    _____

3. Write out Psalm 56:3-4. Now, write it on your heart.

    _____

    _____

    _____

    _____

~ Journal ~

Charles Spurgeon once said, "When I am perfect in faith, I shall be perfect in everything else." Are you exercising and strengthening your faith daily? What can you do today to replace all your fear with faith? How will you apply God's promises to your life?

_____

_____

_____

_____

_____

_____

_____

_____

_____

_____

_____

_____

_____

_____

_____

_____

_____

_____

The Fall Of A Sparrow

~~~

There is special providence in the fall of a sparrow.
If it be now, 'tis not to come; if it be not to come, it
will be now; if it be not now, yet it will come — the
readiness is all. Since no man, of aught he leaves,
knows what is't to leave betimes, let be.

Hamlet
~ Shakespeare

~~~

Hamlet's discussion on whether or not to participate in a fencing match, which probably will result in his death, illustrates that he believes God is in control of his life as well as his death, regardless if he attends or not. Hamlet no longer fears death, now or in the future, because he has come to realize that his destiny rests in God's hands.

His courageous actions prove that he truly believes Jesus' words in Matthew 10:28-29, *"Do not be afraid of those who kill the body but cannot kill the soul. Rather, be afraid of the One who can destroy both soul and body in hell. Are not two sparrows sold for a penny? Yet not one of them will fall to the ground apart from the will of your Father."* God is all supreme and sovereign. He is in complete control of the universe, even the small, insignificant bird. Indeed, there is special providence in the fall of a sparrow.

We, like Hamlet, also do not possess knowledge regarding the specifics of our death. Our future is unknown. We, therefore, must simply and completely trust God. Consequently, Hamlet's words, "The readiness is all" explain the only relevant aspect of death - a right heart.

The Eternal Goodness

I know not where His islands lift
    Their fronded palms in air;
I only know I cannot drift
    Beyond His love and care.
O brothers! If my faith is vain,
    If hopes like these betray.
Pray for me that my feet may gain
    The sure and safer way.
And Thou, O Lord! by whom are seen
    Thy creatures as they be,
Forgive me if too close I lean
    My human heart on Thee.
~ Whittier

Resolve not to forget God. Step out in faith and live without fear or dread. Trust God with everything in your life, remembering the readiness is all.

~ Life Application ~

The earth is the Lord's,
and everything in it,
the world, and all who live in it;
Psalm 24:1

1. First Peter 5:6-7 states: *Humble yourselves, therefore, under God's mighty hand, that he may lift you up in due time. Cast all your anxiety on him because he cares for you.* Write down your fears and burdens to the Lord. Cast them on Him.

    _____

    _____

    _____

    _____

2. Read Psalm 73:26-28. What does the psalmist say about his life on earth? What does he say about God?

    _____

    _____

    _____

    _____

3. Read Isaiah 40:12-26. What do these verses say about God's omniscience? Now read Matthew 10:29-31. How does the Creator feel about you?

    _____

    _____

    _____

~ Journal ~

Can papyrus grow tall where there is no marsh?
  Can reeds thrive without water?
While still growing and uncut,
  they wither more quickly than grass.
Such is the destiny of all who forget God.
  So perishes the hope of the godless.

Job 8:11-13

Are you like the reed withering without water? Have you forgotten God? Do you continuously make decisions based on fear and self-reliance? Write a prayer of devotion and obedient faith to the Lord. Entrust your destiny into His hands.

_____

_____

_____

_____

_____

_____

_____

_____

_____

_____

_____

_____

_____

Hope And A Future

~~~

There is no pit so deep that the love of God is not deeper still.

~ Corrie ten Boom

~~~

Corrie ten Boom realized her life had a special purpose and plan when she was released from a Nazi death camp by a clerical error, and days later, all in the camp were sent to the gas chamber. Corrie knew deep in her heart that her survival was no accident, and she prayerfully asked God, "Why do I, the least deserving, remain?"[4] In her search to understand why only she was spared, Corrie found God's will for her life. She took God's message of love and hope and shared it with the world, devoting her life to writing books and traveling from country to country to speak. Amazingly, Corrie faithfully allowed God to use all the events of her life to accomplish His ultimate plan. She chose to make the best of the most horrific circumstances by keeping her focus on God.

We may never experience such intense heartache, nor may we ever speak before thousands; however, our purpose is no less important that Corrie's. When we respond to God's call as Corrie did, He will restore us emotionally and physically from our suffering to help us ascertain His plan for our life. Even our heartaches will work for our good if we continue to remember that no pit is too deep for God.

The Light of Eternal Love

And I press on with a lighter heart
Through all the ways of the endless rings.
The pure word of the living God
Moves in the depths of them and sings.

Unhampered now by fierce desire
We follow and find no ending here
Till in the light of eternal love
We melt, we disappear.
~ Johann Wolfgang von Goethe
German poet, playwright, novelist

Search for your special purpose in God. Let the light of His eternal love inspire you to fulfill His plans and prosper your life.

Read *The Hiding Place* — Corrie's powerful story on surviving the Holocaust. If you have never read it, you have missed a blessing. Her courage and faith will amaze and encourage you.

I know the plans I have for you, declares the Lord, plans to prosper you and not to harm you, plans to give you hope and a future. Jeremiah 29:11

~ Life Application ~

1. Lamentations 3:25-27 states: *The Lord is good to those whose hope is in him, to the one who seeks him; it is good to wait quietly for the salvation of the Lord. It is good for a man to bear the yoke while he is young.* Affliction can be good for us if we bear it properly, for it can teach submission, patience, and total reliance on God. What do verses 31-33 and 37-38 add?

   _____

   _____

   _____

2. Jeremiah 31:17 states: *There is hope for your future, declares the Lord.* What does Deuteronomy 4:31 promise?

   _____

   _____

   _____

3. What do Job 8:7 and Psalm 40:5 also promise? Apply these verses to your life.

   _____

   _____

   _____

   In Isaiah 61:3, God promises to *bestow a crown of beauty instead of ashes, the oil of gladness instead of mourning, and a garment of praise instead of a spirit of despair.* As God restored Corrie's loss of friends and family, so will He also restore you.

~ Journal ~

Those who hope in the Lord will renew their strength.
They will soar on wings like eagles.

Isaiah 40:31

Remember a specific time in your life when Jesus healed your
broken heart and lifted you from the ashes of grief. How will you
wear your crown of beauty for others to see evidence of Him?

_____

_____

_____

_____

_____

_____

_____

_____

_____

_____

_____

_____

_____

_____

_____

_____

_____

_____

The Treasure Of You

~~~

I celebrate myself, and sing myself.
~ Walt Whitman

~~~

St. Augustine once wrote:

People travel to wonder at the height of mountains,
at the huge waves of the sea,
at the long courses of rivers,
at the vast compass of the ocean,
at the circular motion of the stars,
and they pass by themselves without ever wondering.

Truly, man is the workmanship of God. Only He could create each one of us so vastly different. Only He could construct each one of us into a one-of-a-kind design.

Geneticists' research shows that the odds that your parents could produce another child just like you with your exact DNA material are 1 in 10-to-the-two-billionth power.

You are truly a unique creation — a fearfully and wonderfully designed masterpiece. God made you specifically, created you exactly as you are, for His purposes.

The Creator of the Universe has a personal message for you in Psalm 139. Read verses 13-18, inserting your name, and know that He has great love and concern for your life.

For you created my inmost being;
    you knit me together in my mother's womb.
I praise you because I am fearfully and wonderfully made;
    your works are wonderful,
    I know that full well.
My frame was not hidden from you
    when I was made in the secret place.
When I was woven together in the depths of the earth,
    your eyes saw my unformed body.
All the days ordained for me
    were written in your book
    before one of them came to be.
How precious to me are your thoughts, O God!
    How vast is the sum of them!
Were I to count them,
    they would outnumber the grains of sand.
When I awake,
    I am still with you.

Did you know that God purposefully gave life to your unformed body, that His loving hands literally knit you together in your mother's womb? There is nothing about you that surprises God, for He has intimate and perfect knowledge of your every thought, emotion, and action. Even still, your life is precious and honored in His sight, and His many thoughts toward you are loving.

How do you view yourself? You must strive to see yourself as God sees you — a beautiful creation — a treasure, precious and extraordinary, precisely designed for His pleasure. You should feel free to treasure yourself — to sing and celebrate your life. Learn to be yourself and to love yourself just the way you are.

~ Life Application ~

1. Jeremiah 1:1 states: *"Before I formed you in the womb, I knew you; beforeyou were born I set you apart."* Indeed, God created you specifically and purposefully. What does this verse mean to you, personally — for what do you believe God set you apart?

   _____

   _____

   _____

2. Isaiah 43:4, 10 state: *Since you are precious and honored in my sight, and because I love you...You are...my servant whom I have chosen so that you may know and believe me and understand that I am he.* Read Job 10:10-12. God has bestowed upon you a wonderful gift — the gift of life. He also blesses you with great kindness through His promise to nourish and sustain your spirit. Now write out Isaiah 43:7, and insert your name as you claim God's promises for your life.

   _____

   _____

   _____

3. What does Ephesians 2:10 mean to you? How will you apply this truth to your life?

   _____

   _____

   _____

~ Journal ~

I praise you because I am fearfully and wonderfully made;
your works are wonderful. Psalm 139:14

Celebrate and sing your uniqueness. Thank God for creating you just the way you are. List the positive qualities and traits that He bestowed upon you. Celebrate them. Then, determine how you will use them for God.

_____

_____

_____

_____

_____

_____

_____

_____

_____

_____

_____

_____

_____

_____

_____

A Good Name

~~≈~~

The purest treasure mortal times afford
is spotless reputation.
Richard II
~ Shakespeare

~~≈~~

Psalm 112:6 states: *A righteous man will be remembered forever*. The opposite is also true. Consider the name of Benedict Arnold, the Revolutionary War leader who betrayed America. His name is synonymous with the word "traitor." Yet, what most don't realize is that before Arnold betrayed America, he fought bravely and helped the Continental Army win important battles. He was especially instrumental in winning the battle of Saratoga — a battle which was the turning point in the war, as well as in Arnold's life. Arnold nearly lost his life at Saratoga. He was shot in the leg, and his horse was shot out from under him. Incredibly, if Arnold had died the day he was wounded, he would today be remembered as a great hero instead of a traitor. History books would glorify the name Benedict Arnold.

Shakespeare's wise words on the importance of

reputation seem appropriate.

> Good name in man and woman, dear my lord,
> Is the immediate jewel of their souls;
> Who steals my purse steals trash; 'tis something, nothing;
> 'Twas mine, 'tis his, and has been slave to thousands;
> But he that filches from me my good name
> Robs me of that which not enriches him,
> And makes me poor indeed.
>
> Othello

Incidentally, Arnold received a sum of around £6,000 and a general's commission in the British army. Although his betrayal was for England's sake, British society shunned him, and the British army never trusted him with anything of importance. He died deeply in debt.

Arnold's life teaches us an important lesson: Our lives are a sum of the choices we have made.

Your name is the sum total of your life and is the legacy you leave behind. Treasure your reputation — keep your legacy foremost in your mind while making the choices of your life. Contemplate your name. What is the sum total of your life?

> *A good name is more desirable than great riches;*
> *to be esteemed is better than silver or gold.*
>
> Proverbs 22:1

~ Life Application ~

1. Proverbs 10:7 states: *The memory of the righteous will be a blessing, but the name of the wicked will rot.* Write a description of the memory you wish to leave behind. How will your memory be a blessing?

   _____

   _____

   _____

   _____

2. Ecclesiastes 7:1 states that *a good name is better than fine perfume.* Read Proverbs 3:1-4. How can you achieve a good name in the sight of God and man?

   _____

   _____

   _____

   _____

3. Song of Songs 1:3 states: *Your name is like perfume poured out.* Read 3 John 3-8. These verses speak of the joy of a good reputation and how the early Christians poured out God's sweet fragrance for the "sake of the Name." Is your name like perfume poured out? How will you spread God's sweet fragrance?

   _____

   _____

   _____

∼ Journal ∼

Contemplate your name and reputation. What is the sum total of your life? What have you accomplished in the name of Christ? What do you intend to add to your reputation in the coming year? In five years?

_____

_____

_____

_____

_____

_____

_____

_____

_____

_____

_____

_____

_____

_____

_____

_____

_____

_____

_____

Courage Guarantees

~~~

If one advances confidently in the direction of his
dreams, and endeavors to live the life which he has
imagined, he will meet with a success unexpected
in common hours.

> ~ Henry David Thoreau (1817-1862)
> U.S. philosopher

~~~

Failed in business in 1831.
Defeated for Legislature in 1832.
Second failure in business in 1833.
Suffered nervous breakdown in 1836.
Defeated for Speaker in 1838.
Defeated for Elector in 1840.
Defeated for Congress in 1843.
Defeated for Congress in 1848.
Defeated for Senate in 1855.
Defeated for Vice President in 1856.
Defeated for Senate in 1858.
Elected President in 1860.

Such was Abraham Lincoln's 30-year journey to the
White House. What would motivate a man to continue
following his dreams after suffering so much defeat and
failure? Lincoln did not fear failure. Lincoln persevered

to become a great leader, known for integrity and honor, because he was truly courageous. He rose from defeat time after time because he learned to conquer his fears and to use failure as an opportunity to grow in his dreams — to confidently live the life which he had imagined. He was faithful to display this rare and quiet courage throughout all his life, especially in times of great adversity. While feeling the incredible stress and pressures of leading a divided nation, he spoke these words:

> The possibility that we may fail in the struggle ought not to deter us from the support of a cause we believe to be just.

Former British Prime Minister Winston Churchill once said, "Courage is the first of human qualities because it is the quality which guarantees all the others."

Have you allowed the fear of failure to keep you from following your dreams and achieving your life's destiny? Are you endeavoring to live the life you've imagined?

Strive to be faithful and courageous; adhere to what is true and right, especially in the face of adversity. Pray each day for God's help in overcoming your fears — to help you rise above failure and adversity, so you may learn and grow from them and reach your God-given potential.

~ Life Application ~

Do not fear, for I am with you;
  do not be dismayed, for I am your God.
I will strengthen you and help you;
  I will uphold you with my righteous right hand.
                                    Isaiah 41:10

1. Ephesians 3:20 states: *Now to him who is able to do immeasurably more than all we ask or imagine, according to his power that is at work within us.* Read Romans 8:31-32 and Jeremiah 32:17. Why do we not need to fear failure? What does His Word promise?

    _____

    _____

    _____

2. What does Galatians 6:9 say about giving up? Write this verse down and apply it to your heart.

    _____

    _____

    _____

3. Read 1 Corinthians 2:1-5. How did Paul overcome his weakness and fear?

    _____

    _____

    _____

~ Journal ~

Do you have a dream that as yet you have only imagined? Have you allowed adversity and the fear of failure to limit your potential and keep you from God's plan for your life? Talk honestly to God about it, and see if it's time to head in that direction. Ask Him for the courage and fortitude to live the life He has planned for you. Remember, nothing is too difficult for Him!

_____

_____

_____

_____

_____

_____

_____

_____

_____

_____

_____

_____

_____

_____

_____

_____

Believing Souls

~∿~

Now, God be praised, that to
believing souls
Gives light in darkness, comfort in despair.
~ Shakespeare

~∿~

The Living Bible states in Psalm 34:18 that the *"Lord is close to those whose hearts are breaking."* We only have to draw near to the Great Comforter to receive an abundance of strength and consolation, for Christ understands our sorrow. He sympathizes with us because He experienced suffering and grief firsthand. It is His earnest desire that we cast our burdens on Him — that we trust in Him alone to light our darkness and comfort our despair. Hence a few stanzas from British poet William Blake's poem:

On Another's Sorrow
He doth give his joy to all;
He becomes an infant small;
He becomes a man of woe;
He doth feel the sorrow too.

Think not thou canst sigh a sigh,
And thy maker is not by;
Think not thou canst weep a tear
And thy maker is not near.

O! he gives to us his joy
That our grief he may destroy;
Till our grief is fled and gone
He doth sit by us and moan.

Most Certainly, Christ dwells with us in our darkest moments. Yet, often we fall so deep into our grief that we simply don't recognize His comforting presence. Christ becomes a man of woe and feels all our sorrows. "Think not thou canst weep a tear/ And thy Maker is not near." *The Living Bible* states, *"You have collected all my tears and preserved them in your bottle! You have recorded every one in your book"* (Psalm 56:8). What a comforting thought! We cannot shed one tear that He doesn't know or care about. For as long as we feel sorrow, He will literally sit by us and moan.

Do you not know?
*   Have you not heard?*
The Lord is the everlasting God,
*   the Creator of the ends of the earth.*
He will not grow tired or weary,
*   and his understanding no one can fathom.*
He gives strength to the weary,
*   and increases the power of the weak.*
Isaiah 40:28-29

Trust God with your grief. Let Him share in your sorrow and pour out His healing on you.

~ Life Application ~

1. Psalm 126:5-6 states: *Those who sow in tears will reap with
    songs of joy. He who goes out weeping, carrying seed to sow,
    will return with songs of joy, carrying sheaves with him.* What
    does Isaiah 25:8 also say about your tears?

    _____

    _____

    _____

    _____

2. Write down the promises of Psalm 37:39-40. What do they
    mean to you?

    _____

    _____

    _____

    _____

3. Exodus 15:2 states: *The Lord is my strength and my song;
    he has become my salvation. He is my God, and I will praise
    him, my father's God, and I will exalt him.* Read II Samuel
    22:7, 17. What should you do when in sorrow? How will
    God respond?

    _____

    _____

    _____

    _____

~ Journal ~

The care of God for us is a great thing, if a man believes it at heart: it plucks the burden of sorrow from him.

~ Euripides

Cite a time when Christ sat by your side and grieved with you. Thank Him for his unconditional love and compassion.

_____

_____

_____

_____

_____

_____

_____

_____

_____

_____

_____

_____

_____

_____

_____

_____

_____

Contented I Will Be

~≈~

Content makes poor men rich;
discontent makes rich men poor.
~ Ben Franklin (1706-1790)
American writer, statesman

~≈~

The 17th Century British poet John Dryden once said, "Content is wealth, the riches of the mind, and happy he who can such riches find." How does a person go about finding such riches of contentment — such happiness and satisfaction in life? We begin by understanding that a contented life is not free from frustration and heartache, but it is a life that doesn't allow heartache and frustration to disturb it and steal its joy. When we are truly contented, we exist in a state of peace with God — a state of enjoyment and appreciation for all life's gifts. First Timothy 6:6 states: *Godliness with contentment is great gain.* Truly godly people have the ability to find joy and contentment in this world — whatever the conditions.

Consider the life of Fanny Crosby, blind at the age of six weeks due to errant medical treatment. Instead of grieving her disability and falling into self-pity and bitterness, she found contentment by viewing her blindness as a gift from God. She once said,

> It seemed intended by the blessed providence of God that I should be blind all my life, and I thank Him for the dispensation. If perfect earthly sight were offered me tomorrow, I would not accept it. I might not have sung hymns to the praise of God if I had been distracted by the beautiful and interesting things about me.

Hence, a verse from one of the 8,000 songs written during her 88 years of life.

> Oh what a happy soul I am
> Although I cannot see!
> I am resolved that in this world
> Contented I will be…
>
> How many blessings I enjoy
> That other people don't;
> To weep and sigh because I'm blind,
> I cannot and I won't.
> Age 8

Fortify your heart with godliness and contentment by living as Fanny Crosby — view everything in life as a gift from God.

> *A heart at peace gives life to the body.*
> Proverbs 14:30

~ Life Application ~

1. Proverbs 17:22: *A cheerful heart is good medicine, but a crushed spirit dries up the bones.* What does Hebrews 13:5 promise that should give us a cheerful heart?

   _____

   _____

   _____

   _____

   _____

2. Write 1 Timothy 6:6-10 in your own words.

   _____

   _____

   _____

   _____

   _____

3. Shakespeare once said, "Content is our best having." What does Philippians 4:11-12 say about contentment?

   _____

   _____

   _____

   _____

~ Journal ~

Strive daily to learn the secret of contentment. Paul learned it. He found true peace in all circumstances, *whether well fed or hungry, whether living in plenty or want.* He learned to trust God completely and to respond to Him faithfully with total dependence on Him for strength to accomplish anything. Have you learned the secret of contentment? Have you learned to be content in any and every situation? Is there an area of your heart in which you are discontented? Seek forgiveness and a renewed perspective from God. Ask God to teach you His secret of contentment.

_____

_____

_____

_____

_____

_____

_____

_____

_____

_____

_____

_____

Your Hand, Lord Jesus

~∾~

God shall be my hope,
My stay, my guide and
Lantern to my feet.
~ Shakespeare

~∾~

Matthew 14:29-31 illustrates the miracle of pure faith weakened by fear and doubt: *"Come," he [Jesus] said. Then Peter got down out of the boat, walked on the water and came toward Jesus. But when he saw the wind, he was afraid and, beginning to sink, cried out, "Lord, save me!" Immediately Jesus reached out his hand and caught him. "You of little faith," he said, "why did you doubt?"* Peter's experience reminds us that if we are to truly make God the hope and guide of our life, we must place our total confidence in Him and venture to go without fear wherever He leads. Through His strength and power, we can learn to depend on Him and trust Him completely — we can literally walk on water with Him. Yet, when we allow fear to grip our hearts, our circumstances become greater than our weakened faith, and we begin to sink. Just as Jesus reached out His hand to save Peter from his unbelief, He promises to reach out to us and never let us fall. Peter reminds us that we cannot take our eyes off Jesus for a minute, for waves of fear and winds of doubt can easily overtake us.

Your Hand, Lord Jesus

We receive everything from your hand, Lord Jesus.
Your powerful hand stretches forth
and turns worldly wisdom into holy folly.
Your gentle hand opens and offers
the gift of inner peace.
If ever it seems that your reach is shortened,
it is only to increase our faith and trust,
that we may reach out to you.
And if ever it seems that your hand
is withheld from us,
we know that it is only to conceal
the eternal blessing you have promised —
that we may yearn for that blessing
even more fervently.
~ Soren Kierkegaard
Danish philosopher (1813-1855)

Isaiah 49:15-16 states: *I will not forget you! See, I have engraved you on the palms of my hands.* Be assured that God's hand is stretched out to you to keep you from sinking. Confidently reach out with a strong faith and take hold of His strength and power. "Be not afraid" — in the storms of your life — of the wind and the waves that brew about you. Never take your eyes off His love.

～ Life Application ～

I am the Lord, your God, who takes hold of your right
hand and says to you, Do not fear; I will help you.
Isaiah 41:13

1. Psalm 73:23 states: *Yet I am always with you; you hold me*
    by my right hand. You guide me with your counsel, and
    afterward you will take me into glory. God promises to never
    let you go. Ever! His hand will hold you even unto eternity.
    Thank God for His wonderful, eternal grace and love.

    _____

    _____

    _____

    _____

2. What does God command us in Joshua 1:9? Why?

    _____

    _____

    _____

    _____

    _____

3. Read Psalm 118:6. Put this verse in your own words.

    _____

    _____

    _____

    _____

～Journal ～

Contemplate your relationship with God. Are you walking by faith and courage, or sinking from unbelief and fear? Is a particular fear or worry keeping you from holding on to God's hand? Write in your journal a prayer of confidence to God, trusting that His power will stretch forth to you.

_____

_____

_____

_____

_____

_____

_____

_____

_____

_____

_____

_____

_____

_____

_____

_____

_____

Peace Of God

~~~

My times are in thy hand:
O God, I wish them there;
My life, my friends, my soul,
I leave entirely to thy care.
~ William Lloyd

~~~

Horatio Spafford truly understood the peace of God — the peace that transcends all human understanding. Just days after a shipwreck took the lives of his four young daughters, Spafford replied with remarkable serenity, "It is well — God's will be done."

Shortly after his great loss, while viewing the location where the tragedy occurred, he wrote a hymn which is still sung today.

The following is a stanza from Spafford's heartfelt testament to his faith in God:

When peace like a river attendeth my way,
When sorrows like sea billows roll;
Whatever my lot,
Thou has taught me to say,
"It is well, it is well with my soul."

Isaiah 43:2, 4 tell us that God promises to stand beside

us and sustain us in times of our greatest trials:

When you pass through the waters, I will be with you; and when you pass through the rivers, they will not sweep over you. When you walk through the fire, you will not be burned; the flames will not set you ablaze....Since you are precious and honored in my sight, and because I love you.

Spafford's unfathomable peace can also be ours to sustain us in our greatest sorrows. It begins with the realization that our strength can never be enough, and a commitment to wholly rely on God. When we cast all our burdens on Him and entrust absolutely everything in our lives to His care, our souls experience such ease, such complete serenity and inner tranquillity, to rise above our heartache.

Trust God in your times of heartache. Place your sorrow in His hands, and He will turn your suffering into good — He will perfect you and heal you and make you whole. Always remember the words of Charles Spurgeon: "The joys of heaven will surely compensate for the sorrows of earth."

And the peace of God, which transcends all understanding, will guard your hearts and your minds in Christ Jesus.

Philippians 4:7

～ Life Application ～

1. Isaiah 57: 18-19 states: *I will heal him; I will guide him and restore comfort to him, creating praise on the lips of the mourners in Israel. Peace, peace, to those far and near, says the Lord. And I will heal them.* Read John 14:27. What does Jesus promise? How should we respond to this promise?

   _____

   _____

   _____

   _____

   _____

2. Write down the promises of Nahum 1:7 and Psalm 71:20. Then, write these words on your heart.

   _____

   _____

   _____

   _____

3. What do Romans 8:17-18 say about our sufferings?

   _____

   _____

   _____

   _____

   _____

~ Journal ~

Write about a time in your life when you suffered and experienced God's peace firsthand. If you didn't feel an inner serenity, write a prayer of commitment to wholly rely on God. Ask Him to fill you with His peace and rest.

_____

_____

_____

_____

_____

_____

_____

_____

_____

_____

_____

_____

_____

_____

_____

_____

_____

_____

Greater Love

~~~

Love is like a violin.
The music may stop now and then,
but the strings remain forever.
~ Bacher

~~~

In World War II, Maximillian Kolbe, a Polish priest under the Franciscan order, took in and cared for thousands of Polish Jews. Kolbe quickly became a marked man, and was arrested in 1941 and sent to a concentration camp. While in prison, he comforted many, sharing his food, his bunk, his love and his faith in Christ. He even prayed for his captors.

Then came the fateful day when a prisoner escaped from cell block fourteen. The Nazis randomly selected ten prisoners to kill as punishment. Francis Gajowniczek, a man unknown to Kolbe, was one of the ten chosen that day. Thinking of his wife and children, a weeping Gajowniczek begged and pleaded for his life. But the Nazis ignored his pleas and prepared to take the victims to a cell where they would be denied food and water until they died.

In an unconditional act of charity, Father Kolbe

stepped forward and asked to speak to the commander. Miraculously, he wasn't shot on the spot; prisoners were not allowed to speak or move without permission.

With great calm, Father Kolbe requested to die in the place of Gajowniczek. He had no wife and children, he told the commandant; he was old and not good for anything. Besides, the other prisoner was in better condition.

Kolbe's request was granted and he was allowed to take Gajowniczek's place. He outlived the other nine prisoners, dying only after his heart was injected with phenol.

Gajowniczek later said he had been stunned that someone else willingly and voluntarily offered his life for him, a stranger. Gajowniczek lived a long and full life, forever grateful and indebted to Kolbe. Every year he returned to Auschwitz to pay tribute and say thank you to the man who died in his place.

By his sacrifice, Father Kolbe demonstrated the ultimate act of Christ-like love. Truly, the strings of his love and the sacrifice he made in the name of love will live forever.

Greater love has no one than this, that he lay down his life for his friends. John 15:13

~ Life Application ~

1. Isaiah 53:6-7, 12 state: *We all, like sheep, have gone astray, each of us has turned to his own way; and the Lord has laid on him the iniquity of us all. He was oppressed and afflicted, yet he did not open his mouth; he was led like a lamb to the slaughter....For he bore the sin of many, and made intercession for the transgressors.* How do these verses make you feel? Today, give thanks to Jesus for laying down His life for you.

   _____

   _____

   _____

   _____

   _____

2. Read 1 John 4:7-12. Put those verses in your own words.

   _____

   _____

   _____

   _____

3. What does Ephesians 5:1-2 command you to do?

   _____

   _____

   _____

   _____

~ Journal ~

Father Kolbe's legacy remains today. He raised the standard of love through his selfless sacrifice. How have you raised the standard of love? What is the most selfless act you have ever done in the name of love? Pay tribute to and give thanks to the man who died in your place. Thank Him for His sacrifice.

_____

_____

_____

_____

_____

_____

_____

_____

_____

_____

_____

_____

_____

_____

_____

_____

_____

Love Is

~~~~~

Love is anterior to life,
Posterior to death,
Initial of creation, and
The exponent of breath
~ Emily Dickinson

~~~~~

Love is the very essence of God, for God is love. His love is everywhere: *in the heavens...in the depths...on the wings of the dawn...on the far side of the sea* (Psalm 139). We can never escape God, for His love fills the universe entirely. Surrounded by God's unfailing and enduring mercy, we are safe in Love. The Psalmist described it like this: *"Thou hast beset me behind and before, and laid thine hand upon me"* (Psalm 139:5 KJV). Indeed, we can never be removed from God's lovingkindness and care because Love precedes us and follows us to hem us in, encompassing us with His protection, and ever guiding us in the way everlasting.

God demonstrates His wonderful love for you every moment. "Initial of creation," Love cared for you, knew you, and set you apart before you were even born, purposefully and specifically planning your life before creation. Love orchestrated your very existence by knitting together your soul in the womb and breathing life into you. In addition, Love divinely and sovereignly ordained each and every day of your life before even one of them came to be. So awesome is God's omnipotence that He understands you perfectly and searches your heart to know you completely. Just the thought that Love represented you in sacrifice to speak on your behalf, to infinitely and perpetually provide love to you, before creation and into eternity, should fill you with awe and thankfulness.

Celebrate God's love. Claim the rewards and treasures of His promises for your life. Enjoy His protecting, abiding, prospering, caring and everlasting love.

> O Lord, you have searched me
>   and you know me.
> You know when I sit and when I rise;
>   you perceive my thoughts from afar.
> You discern my going out and my lying down;
>   you are familiar with all my ways.
> Before a word is on my tongue
>   you know it completely, O Lord.
> You hem me in—behind and before;
>   you have laid your hand upon me.
> Such knowledge is too wonderful for me,
>   too lofty for me to attain.
> Where can I go from your Spirit?
>   Where can I flee from your presence?
> If I go up to the heavens, you are there;
>   if I make my bed in the depths, you are there.
> If I rise on the wings of the dawn,
>   if I settle on the far side of the sea,
> even there your hand will guide me,
>   your right hand will hold me fast....Psalm 139:1-12

~ Life Application ~

1. The Lord appeared to us in the past saying, "I have loved you with an everlasting love." Jeremiah 3:13. What has love done to your past? Read Isaiah 43:25 to answer.

   _____

   _____

   _____

   _____

2. How will love help you live your present life? First Corinthians 2:9 states: *No eye has seen, no ear has heard, no mind has conceived what God has prepared for those who love him.* Paul goes on to say in verse 10, *but God has revealed it to us by his Spirit.* Now read verses 11-16 to answer how love is your present.

   _____

   _____

   _____

   _____

3. What is your future in the love of Christ? First John 3:1 states: *How great is the love the Father has lavished on us, that we should be called children of God.* Read verses 2 and 3 to answer.

   _____

   _____

   _____

~ Journal ~

How priceless is your unfailing love!

Psalm 36:7

Meditate on God's enduring and unfailing love. Write your own thoughts on God's omniscience, on your admiration and appreciation of God. Thank Him for His great care and concern for every detail of your life — for loving you in your past, present, and future.

_____

_____

_____

_____

_____

_____

_____

_____

_____

_____

_____

_____

_____

_____

_____

_____

_____

Love Praying

~∾~

Intercession is basically love praying. In the very truest sense, intercession is love on its knees.
~ Dick Eastman

~∾~

We honestly cannot do more for a person and make a greater difference in a life than to pray. When we take the needs of others to heart and petition God on their behalf, God will hear us and touch their lives through our prayers. Abraham Lincoln said this about intercessory prayer: "I remember my mother's prayers and they have followed me. They have clung to me all my life." These are remarkable words, considering his mother died when he was only eight. Intercessory prayer is an excellent way to lay hold of the promises of God — to literally put love for someone into action. So powerful is this priceless privilege, its effects can last a lifetime!

John Calvin, the 16th Century French theologian and reformer, said this:

> Our prayer must not be self-centered. It must arise not only because we feel our own need as a burden

which we must lay upon God, but also because we are bound up in love for our fellow men that we feel their need as acutely as our own. To make intercession for men is the most powerful and practical way in which we can express our love for them.

Do you regularly express your love for others by lifting your hands in prayer for them? Today, intercede for those in need. Unselfishly set aside your needs and make a contribution to the life of another by lifting him in prayer to God.

Hands of Prayer
More things are wrought by prayer
Than this world dreams of. Wherefore, let thy voice
Rise like a fountain for me night and day.
For what are men better than sheep or goats
That nourish a blind life within the brain,
If, knowing God, they lift not hands of prayer
Both for themselves and those who call them friend?
For so the whole round earth is every way
Bound by gold chains about the feet of God.
~ Tennyson (from Morte d'Arthur)

Pray one for another... The effectual fervent prayer of a righteous man availeth much.
James 5:16 (KJV)

~ Life Application ~

1. Read James 5:13-18. When does James say intercessory prayer is appropriate? How should we pray?

    _____

    _____

    _____

    _____

2. Read Romans 15:30-31. For what does Paul ask? Why?

    _____

    _____

    _____

3. Isaiah 62:6-7 states: *I have posted watchmen on your walls, O Jerusalem; they will never be silent day or night. You who call on the Lord, give yourselves no rest, and give him no rest....* For whom will you pray? What are his or her needs? Be their "watchman on the wall," by writing the names of those for whom you wish to pray and include the reasons you are interceding.

    _____

    _____

    _____

    _____

~ Journal ~

Prayers for men are far more important than prayers
for things because men more deeply concern God's
will and the work of Jesus Christ than things.
                                              E.M. Bounds

Write your prayers of intercession. Be sure to include today's
date, so you can reference this prayer upon its answer.

_____

_____

_____

_____

_____

_____

_____

_____

_____

_____

_____

_____

_____

_____

_____

Worthy Purpose

~∾~

Many persons have a wrong idea of what constitutes true happiness, it is not attained through self-gratification but through fidelity to a worthy purpose.

~ Helen Keller

~∾~

The Bible states: *The things you planned for us no one can recount to you...plans to prosper and not harm us. Plans to give us hope and a future* (Psalm 40:5; Jeremiah 29:11). God has designs of greatness for each of our lives — a specific plan to prosper us with grace, to give us hope and a future of everlasting love. Our minds simply cannot conceive all that God has in store for our lives. To lay hold of His marvelous blessings, we must strive to understand God's purposes by seeking His truths and will. We each must live our life and praise Him in our own unique way, for when we are committed to Him and properly motivated by faith, hope, and love, He will surely give us the desires of our hearts to make all our plans succeed.[5]

Today, make it your determined purpose to know God. Ask Him to *"fill you with the knowledge of his will through all spiritual wisdom and understanding...to help you live a life worthy of him to please him in every way"* (Colossians 1:9-10).

Contemplate Phillips Brooks' inspirational and poignant metaphor on living the richest and brightest life:

Voyage

Think of life as a voyage.
The truest liver of the truest life
is like a voyager who, as he sails,
is not indifferent to all the beauty of the sea around him.
The morning and the evening sun,
the moonlight and the starlight,
the endless change of the vast water that he floats on,
the passing back and forth of other ships
between him and the sky,
the incidents and company on his own vessel —
all these are pleasant to him;
but their pleasure is borne up by
and woven in with
his interest in the purpose for which he undertook the voyage.
That lies beyond and that lies under the voyage all the while.
He is not sailing just for the sake of sailing.
He would never have undertaken the voyage for his own sake.
Another man,
who has no purpose beyond the voyage,
is vexed and uneasy.
He is so afraid of not getting the best out of it
that he loses its best.
The spots and imperfections in its pleasure worry him.
Those are the differences of the ways in which men live.
One man forgets his own life
in the purposes for which his life is lived,
and he is the man whose life grows richest and brightest.
Another man is always thinking about himself,
and so never gets beyond himself
into those purposes of living,
out of which all the fullness of personal life may flow back to him.

**Are you sailing for the sake of sailing, or are you living
the richest and brightest life?**

∼ Life Application ∼

My determined purpose is that I may know Him.
Philippians 3:10 (AMP)

1. Psalm 77:19 states: *Your path led through the sea, your way through the mighty waters, though your footprints were not seen.* God desires that we follow His path of righteousness. According to Ephesians 5:17, what is our responsibility during our voyage? Read Psalm 107:23-27. Describe the scene.

    _____

    _____

    _____

    _____

2. What did the people do in their stress? What did the Lord do for them?

    > *Then they cried out to the Lord in their trouble,*
    > *and he brought them out of their distress.*
    > *He stilled the storm to a whisper;*
    > *the waves of the sea were hushed.*
    > *They were glad when it grew calm,*
    > *and he guided them to their desired haven.*
    > *Let them give thanks to the Lord for his unfailing love*
    > *and his wonderful deeds for men.*

    Psalm 107:28-31

3. Be assured, God is in control. Do you depend on Him to still your storms and hush the waves of the sea? Contemplate your heart. Are you a seaworthy vessel in the eyes of the Lord, able to withstand the terrifying and relentless waves of storms? Will you give God the captain's seat and trust Him with your life? Read Proverbs 3:5-6. Write it on your heart.

~ Journal ~

Contemplate the following: Are your pleasures borne up and woven in the purpose of your voyage? Is your voyage navigated by God? Is He the Captain of your life? Jesus once stated, *"Whoever finds his life will lose it, and whoever loses his life for my sake will find it"* (Matthew 10:39). Share in the beauty of the world and all those within it by giving yourself away. Put away selfish desires, and seek God's will for your life. Follow Brook's advice and allow the fullness of your life to flow back to you.

_____

_____

_____

_____

_____

_____

_____

_____

_____

_____

_____

_____

_____

_____

_____

_____

Unfailing Love

~~~

One word frees us of all the weight
And pain of life: that word is love.
~ Sophocles (c. 495-406 B.C.)
Greek playwright

~~~

A few lines from Shakespeare's *Sonnet CXVI* speak of a love that is real and unfailing:

Love is not love
Which alters when it alteration finds,
Or bends with the remover to remove.
O, no! It is an ever-fixed mark
That looks on tempests and is never shaken;
It is the star to every wandering bark,
Whose worths unknown, although his
Height be taken.

God's love is a love like no other love on earth. His love is constant and unchanging — it does not "alter;" it does not "bend." Nor, will He ever "remove" His love from us. There is nothing we can do or say that can make Him love us more or take His love away from us. Absolutely nothing in all creation can separate us from the love of God. He loves us simply because we are His children. Moreover, His love is especially prevalent during the turbulent and violent storms of our lives. Isaiah 54:10 states: *Though the mountains be shaken and the hills be removed, yet my unfailing love for you will not be shaken.* Truly, God's love will never fail us. His love can never be shaken, for it promises to persevere and prevail throughout all eternity to act as an "ever-fixed mark" that can weather any storm to serve as our beacon in times of distress.

Treasure the love that God has so freely and graciously bestowed upon you. Be encouraged by His unfailing, everlasting love.

I am convinced that neither death nor life,
neither angels nor demons,
neither the present nor the future,
nor any powers,
neither height nor depth,
nor anything else in all creation,
will be able to separate us from the love of God
that is in Christ Jesus our Lord.
Romans 8:38-39

~ Life Application ~

1. Deuteronomy 31:6 states: *Be strong and courageous. Do not be afraid or terrified because of them, for the Lord your God goes with you; he will never leave you nor forsake you.* What are your fears? How does His promise make you feel? How will you apply this verse to your life?

   _____

   _____

   _____

   _____

2. Romans 5:8 states: *God demonstrates his own love for us in this: While we were still sinners, Christ died for us.* Today, how will you demonstrate the unfailing, unconditional love of God to others?

   _____

   _____

   _____

   _____

3. Jeremiah 31:3 states: *I have loved you with an everlasting love; I have drawn you with loving-kindness.* What a promise! Write a brief thank-you note to God for the sweet surety of His love.

   _____

   _____

   _____

～ Journal ～

The 19th Century American writer Nathaniel Hawthorne once said, "Just as there comes a warm sunbeam into every cottage window so comes a love — born of God's care for every separate need." God loves you with an unfailing love, a love that cares deeply for your every need, no matter how small. Turn your needs over to God, and allow His true and perfect love to free you from all the weight and pain of life. Let His love restore and refresh your soul.

_____

_____

_____

_____

_____

_____

_____

_____

_____

_____

_____

_____

_____

_____

_____

A New Heart

~~~

Have a heart that never hardens.
~ Charles Dickens

~~~

A hardened heart doesn't listen to God and refuses to stay in His plan. When we repeatedly ignore Him, we eventually become deaf to His will and wander aimlessly with no sense of direction. Our spirits of rebellion and disobedience cause us to suffer. And, needlessly, we miss out on the promise of His blessings — blessings of joy and rest that come only from a pliable, obedient heart. Thus, the words of Hebrews 3:8 remind us to learn from the Israelites and heed God's voice today:

> *Today, if you hear his voice,*
> *do not harden your hearts*
> *as you did in the rebellion,*
> *during the time of testing in the desert.*

The Israelites responded to God's faithfulness with unbelief and disobedience. They distrusted God and murmured ungratefully, despite His marvelous works on their behalf. Just as God desired obedient and faithful hearts from the Israelites, He desires soft, pliable hearts from us. We must allow His Word to strengthen our spirits and renew our minds, so we respond obediently and quickly to His voice. Are you listening for God's voice? How will you respond? Scottish novelist Robert Louis Stevenson wrote a prayer, asking God to awaken his sullen, dead heart:

The Celestial Surgeon

If I have faltered more or less
In my great task of happiness;
If I have moved among my race
And shown no glorious morning face;
If beams from happy human eyes
Have moved me not; if morning skies,
Books, and my food, and summer rain
Knocked on my sullen heart in vain;
Lord, thy most pointed pleasure take
And stab my spirit broad awake;
Or, Lord, if too obdurate I,
Choose thou, before that spirit die,
A piercing pain, a killing sin,
And to my dead heart run them in.

Are you wandering astray in a spiritual desert? Have you hardened your heart to God's voice? God wants you to trust Him — to go to Him and enjoy the blessings of the Promised Land. Respond to His voice today.

~ Life Application ~

I will give you a new heart and put a new spirit in you. I will remove from you your heart of stone. And I will put my spirit in you and move you to follow my decrees.
Ezekiel 36:26-27

1. Ezekiel 18:31 states: *Rid yourselves of all the offenses you have committed, and get a new heart and a new spirit.* Do you have any offensive spirits in your heart of which you need to rid yourself? Confess them to God now. With a contrite heart, ask Him to deliver you into His righteousness.

   _____

   _____

   _____

2. Write a prayer before God of Psalm 51: 10-12, 17.

   _____

   _____

   _____

3. Read Hebrews 3:7-12. Examine your life. Do you have a sinful, unbelieving, and ungrateful heart? Do you continuously test God as the Israelites did on their way out of Egypt? Read Romans 8:5-11. How can you overcome a spirit of disobedience?

   _____

   _____

   _____

~ Journal ~

Search me, O God, and know my heart; test me and know my anxious thoughts. See if there is any offensive way in me, and lead me in the way everlasting. Psalm 139:23-24

Test the integrity of your heart. Ask the Celestial Surgeon to change your heart to pliable flesh and reveal Himself to you by the transforming power of His Spirit.

_____

_____

_____

_____

_____

_____

_____

_____

_____

_____

_____

_____

_____

_____

_____

_____

_____

The Age Of Miracles

~≈~

Miracles are not contrary to nature, but only
contrary to what we know about nature.

St. Augustine

~≈~

Thomas Carlyle once said, "The age of miracles is
forever here." Undoubtedly, miracles occur everyday all
around us. In *All But My Life,* a memoir of surviving the
holocaust, Gerda Weissman shares the incredible and
miraculous tale of a friend from Gruenberg Labor Camp.
Her friend was sent to Auschwitz to die because her x-ray
had shown tuberculosis. A few years later, while visiting a
museum in Germany, Gerda heard a familiar voice: "Isn't
that Gerda? It's me, not my ghost," said a rosy girl in a blue
sweater.

As the young woman came close, Gerda remembered
their sad farewell in Gruenberg before her friend had left
for Auschwitz. As they embraced, they both started to
cry. Then she told Gerda what had happened.

When her group reached Auschwitz they were
taken to the death house, but traffic was heavy there.
Things were so busy, they had to wait for death. As
she sat on the ground, she idly dug into the soil of
which she was soon to become a part. The gesture

was her salvation, for she unearthed a handful of gems. To what forgotten soul had they belonged?

The girl was momentarily dazed. Then she ran up to an SS guard — what had she to lose? "Help me," she pleaded, and gave him the bundle. "I want to live."

Somehow he got her and two other girls from her group places to work in the kitchen. The parcel of gems saved three lives, even though the guard could have taken the gift and refused to help the girls.

When the friend finished her story, Gerda asked her about her lungs.

She smiled, "That is another strange story. I went to a number of doctors, but they found nothing wrong. Perhaps that is another miracle, or perhaps the doctor in Gruenberg made a mistake!"

Whatever the explanation was, the girl had been given back her life.[6]

Miracles are God's expression of His incredible power, a manifestation of His divinity. Even today, God abundantly uses miracles to fulfill His purposes, using whatever means — be it a handful of gems or an x-ray — to bring about what He has planned. Most importantly, God uses miracles to demonstrate His awesome love for us, to reveal Himself, and to prove that He is the one, true God.

For Thou art great, and doest wondrous things:
thou art God alone. Psalm 86:10 (KJV)

~ Life Application ~

1. Jeremiah 32:17 states: *Ah, Sovereign Lord, you have made the heavens and the earth by your great power and outstretched arm. Nothing is too hard for you.* Truly, God can do anything. What does Matthew 19:26 say?

   _____

   _____

   _____

2. Psalm 24:1 states: *The earth is the Lord's, and everything in it, the world, and all who live in it.* God is in control. He holds the world and each one of us in His hands. Read Romans 8:28. Does your love for Him show complete surrender to His purpose? Do you trust in this awesome promise of God? What does this verse mean to you specifically, personally?

   _____

   _____

   _____

3. Write out Psalm 9:1.

   _____

   _____

4. Now tell of His wonders concerning you.

   _____

   _____

~ Journal ~

We must never take God's wondrous acts for granted. Contemplate the words of Longfellow: "Nothing is or can be accidental with God." Write about a miracle that He has done for you — a time when God's hand was clearly evident. Then, take time to praise Him for purposefully placing you exactly where you are today. Thank Him for all that has brought you to this point in time.

_____

_____

_____

_____

_____

_____

_____

_____

_____

_____

_____

_____

_____

_____

_____

_____

_____

Apples of Gold

~∾~

Kind words are short and easy to speak, but their
echoes are truly endless.

~ Mother Teresa (1910-1997)

~∾~

Aptly spoken words are invaluable; they comfort
and soothe, encourage and uplift. When we speak words
of seasonable advice and instruction, our words become
pleasant, *a honeycomb, sweet to the soul and healing to the
bones* (Proverbs 16:24). George William Childs once said:

> Do not keep the alabaster boxes of your love and
> tenderness sealed up until your friends are dead.
> Fill their lives with sweetness. Speak approving,
> cheering words while their ears can hear them, and
> while their hearts can be thrilled and made happier
> by them.

Too often, we forget or simply choose not to share
our love and appreciation with those around us. Sadly,
our pride keeps those we love from ever really knowing
just how wonderful and special they are to us.

Everyone needs inspiration and encouragement. We
should not waste a single opportunity to nourish and
build up another's life, for we may never realize how

desperately an inspiring word is needed at that very moment to help them overcome a secret trial or struggle.

A word is dead
When it is said,
Some say.
I say it just
Begins to live
That day.
~ Emily Dickinson

Indeed, our words will live on if we speak soft, gentle words of healing and encouragement. Ephesians 4:29 states: *Do not let any unwholesome talk come out of your mouths, but only what is helpful for building others up according to their needs that it may benefit those who listen.*

Won't you commit to building up another and making a difference in someone's life by passing on a kindness? Open your alabaster boxes and share the sweetness of your golden apples of encouragement and blessing with those you love.

A word aptly spoken
is like apples of gold
in settings of silver.
Proverbs 25:11

~ Life Application ~

1. Proverbs 10:20-21 states: *The tongue of the righteous is choice silver, but the heart of the wicked is of little value. The lips of the righteous nourish many, but fools die for lack of judgment.* What does Hebrews 10:24-25 say? How will you do this?

   _____

   _____

   _____

   _____

2. John 16:33 (KJV) states: *Be of good cheer; I have overcome the world.* Read Joshua 1:1-7. How did the Lord encourage Joshua after Moses' death? Thank God for His Word and its limitless ability to cheer and challenge you.

   _____

   _____

   _____

   _____

3. What do Ephesians 4:29, 31 & Colossians 4:6 say about our speech?

   _____

   _____

   _____

   _____

~ Journal ~

George McDonald once said, "If instead of a gem, or even a flower, we would cast the gift of a lovely thought into the heart of a friend, that would be giving as the angels give." Whom do you know that needs an "apple of gold"? Write down the gift of inspiring and encouraging words you intend to share and with whom you will share them.

_____

_____

_____

_____

_____

_____

_____

_____

_____

_____

_____

_____

_____

_____

_____

_____

_____

_____

Reap The Fruit Of Love

~∾~

The world is sown with the good, but unless I turn
my glad thoughts into practical living and till my
own field, I cannot reap a kernel of the good.
~ Helen Keller

~∾~

Approximately fifty years before Helen Keller lived,
a woman named Laura Bridgeman, also deaf and blind,
laid the foundation for Helen's inspirational life. Laura
spent hours of painstaking effort, touching raised letters
to learn words and grammar, thus enabling her to be one
of the first with her handicaps to write poetry and books.
It was Laura's perseverance and determination, combined
with her incredible accomplishments that led Annie
Sullivan to study Laura's case in preparation for the
assignment of her first student, Helen Keller.

Charles Dickens wrote of Laura: "This sightless,
earless, voiceless child may teach you lessons you will
do well to follow."

Truly, Laura's life teaches an important lesson — a
lesson of perseverance and determination to sow the seeds
of practical living and turn them into good. And, although

Laura probably never realized how her life helped to improve and change the world for so many people, she didn't let her handicaps stop her from making a contribution. Instead, she simply did her part with what she had to give back generously.

Perseverance

We must not hope to be mowers,
And to gather the ripe gold ears,
Unless we have first been sowers
And watered the furrows with tears.
It is not just as we take it,
This mystical world of ours,
Life's field will yield as we make it
A harvest of thorns or of flowers.
~ Goethe

Let your life send a message to the world. Make it your goal to use the gifts God has given you — to sow your life's field to yield a harvest of flowers.

Sow for yourselves righteousness, reap the fruit of unfailing love, and break up your unplowed ground.
Hosea 10:12

∼ Life Application ∼

1. The last lines of Goethe's poem, "a man reaps what he sows," echo the Bible. Read Galatians 6:7-8. What is your life's field yielding? Contemplate what you want to come back to you tomorrow. Write down some specifics about what you do want to reap and what you do not want to reap from life's field.

   _____

   _____

   _____

2. John 12:24 states: *I tell you the truth, unless a kernel of wheat falls to the ground and dies, it remains only a single seed. But if it dies, it produces many seeds.* One kernel will produce many, but we don't reap what we've sown until much later. What do 2 Corinthians 9:6, 10 and Proverbs 24:30-31 say about the field of life?

   _____

   _____

   _____

3. Psalm 1:3 states: *He is like a tree planted by streams of water, which yields its fruit in season and whose leaf does not wither. Whatever he does prospers.* Claim this verse for your life. Write it here, placing your name in His promise.

   _____

   _____

∼ Journal ∼

Hebrews 6:7 states: *Land that drinks in the rain often falling on it and that produces a crop useful to those for whom it is farmed receives the blessing of God.* Do you drink in God's Word often? Is your life producing the fruits of His love? Consider this: Laura Bridgeman never knew how much her life would influence Helen Keller and the world, just as we may never realize how our smallest deeds touch and change others. We must, therefore, be active in our purpose to "produce a useful crop" to impact all those we can. What seeds will you sow today? How will you turn your practical living into a useful crop?

_____

_____

_____

_____

_____

_____

_____

_____

_____

_____

_____

_____

_____

_____

The Power Of Persistent Prayer

~~~

Never think that God's delays
Are God's denials.
Hold on; hold fast; hold out.
Patience is genius.
~ R.C. Trench

~~~

*O*ften God delays the answers to our prayers to keep us "holding on and holding fast," so we continue asking and seeking Him. God promises good gifts, and He is a rewarder of those who diligently and persistently seek Him in prayer. In *Steps to Christ*, author Ellen G. White states: "Prayer is the key in the hand of faith to unlock heaven's storehouse, where are treasured the boundless resources of Omnipotence." Prayer truly is the key to boundless resources. It leads us directly to God and builds our faith in Him. Consequently, God will sometimes delay the answers to our prayers to test the sincerity of our spirits and to build patience and endurance in our faith. We must be ever watchful for His response because He will surely answer in a way that is best for our lives. C.S. Lewis shared his thoughts on prayer:

Prayer in the sense of petition, asking for things, is a small part of it; confession and penitence are its threshold, adoration its sanctuary, the presence and vision and enjoyment of God its bread and wine. In it God shows himself to us. That He answers prayers is a corollary — not necessarily the most important one — from that revelation. What He does is learned from what He is.

Indeed, what He does is learned from what He is. How might we learn who He is? Jeremiah 33:3 states: *Call unto me, and I will answer thee, and shew thee great and mighty things, which thou knowest not* (KJV). God wants to reveal Himself to us, to provide us with a full assurance of His awesome power. Prayer is an excellent way to lay hold of His promises and to learn who He truly is.

Call on God today. Learn who He is by the great and mighty things He will surely show you.

Ask and it will be given to you;
Seek and you will find;
Knock and the door will be opened to you.
For everyone who asks receives;
He who seeks finds;
And to him who knocks,
The door will be opened.
Matthew 7:7

~ Life Application ~

1. Job 22:27 states: *You will pray to him and he will hear you.*
    Hebrews 11:6 states that we must approach Him with faith.
    *Without faith it is impossible to please God, because anyone
    who comes to him must believe that he exists and that he
    rewards those who earnestly seek him.* What does Colossians
    4:2 say about prayer?

    _____

    _____

    _____

2. James 5:17-18 speak of Elijah's determination and faith in
    prayer. Prayer is a powerful tool. Earnest, persistent prayer
    can have miraculous results. What other incredible feat did
    Elijah's prayers accomplish? Read 1 Kings 18:16-39 to answer.

    _____

    _____

    _____

3. Psalm 31:22 states: *In my alarm I said, "I am cut off from
    your sight!" Yet you heard my cry for mercy when I called to
    you for help.* In times of trouble, we often feel cut off from
    God when answers to our prayers don't come in our
    timing. What do verses 23 and 24 say God will do for us?
    What must we do for Him?

    _____

    _____

    _____

~ Journal ~

Read the parable of the persistent widow in Luke 18:1-5. Let it inspire you to never give up on God and to be persistent in your prayers — to keep **asking, seeking, and knocking.**

Do you have a request that is as yet unanswered? Write a petition to God with confidence and assurance — a prayer of anticipation and expectant belief that He will answer in a way that is best for you.

_____

_____

_____

_____

_____

_____

_____

_____

_____

_____

_____

_____

_____

_____

_____

_____

_____

Sweet Profits

~~◇~~

Sweet are the uses of adversity,
Which, like the toad, ugly and venomous,
Wears yet a precious jewel in his head;
And this our life, exempt from public haunt,
Finds tongues in trees, books in the running brooks,
Sermons in stones, and good in every thing.
Duke Senior *As You Like It*
~ Shakespeare

~~◇~~

Although exiled by his villainous brother, the duke manages to maintain a positive attitude — to consider his suffering to be like an ugly toad with a precious jewel inside. Instead of becoming embittered and focusing on the pain of exile and isolation, he chooses to rejoice in the freedom from society and crowds — to befriend and learn from nature, which he has found to be much simpler and more delightful than life at court. He has found the "sweet uses" of his adversity — contentment in living off the bounty of the land and fulfillment in listening to nature's voice in trees, brooks, and stones.

We must also search for the "sweet uses" of our trials and learn to benefit from them and find contentment in them. Moreover, if we are able to do more than merely survive our trials, we must do as the duke did and choose to find the good in everything.

My Days Go On

I praise Thee while my days go on;
I love Thee while my days go on:
Through dark and dearth, through fire and frost,
With emptied arms and treasure lost,
I thank Thee while my days go on.

Elizabeth Barrett Browning's words are truly wise, for as long as we have breath, in every circumstance and season of life, we must continue to praise and thank God. Most especially when life doesn't seem to be going well, we must search for the good in our situation — seek to find the precious jewel in the ugly toad — and believe that God's divine providence will work all things out for the best.

Rejoice evermore.
Pray without ceasing.
In everything give thanks:
for this is the will of God in Christ Jesus
concerning you.
1 Thessalonians 5:16-18 (KJV)

～ Life Application ～

1. Psalm 68:19 states: *Blessed be the Lord, who daily loadeth us with benefits, even the God of our salvation. Selah.* (KJV) We should daily praise and thank God for all His benefits. Simply thanking Him daily for His blessings will take our focus from our burdens and place it where it belongs — on God. Make a list of the benefits you have received from God.

   _____

   _____

   _____

2. Ephesians 5:19-20 states: *Speak to one another with psalms, hymns, and spiritual songs. Sing and make music in your heart to the Lord, always giving thanks to God the Father for everything, in the name of our Lord Jesus Christ.* Read Acts 16:19-25. In what circumstance did Paul and Silas give thanks and sing spiritual songs? What does this mean to you?

   _____

   _____

   _____

3. Job was certainly a man who praised God, *through dark and dearth, through fire and frost, with emptied arms and treasure lost.* Read Job chapter 1. What earthly treasures did he lose? Note Job's response to his calamity in verses 21-22.

   _____

   _____

~ Journal ~

Do you have an attitude of ingratitude? Is a particular situation or circumstance preventing you from true worship and praise? Confess it to God; then, search for the precious jewel in your ugly toad. Rejoice and give thanks unto God with an attitude of praise and thanksgiving.

_____

_____

_____

_____

_____

_____

_____

_____

_____

_____

_____

_____

_____

_____

_____

The Soul On Its Knees

~∾~

Certain thoughts are prayers. There are
moments when, whatever be the attitude of
the body, the soul is on its knees.

Les Miserables
~ Victor Hugo

~∾~

The story of Hannah is one of the greatest lessons on
the art of prayer. It begins in 1 Samuel 1:10-11 as a prayer
of sorrow and anguish, a desperate plea for a son: *In
bitterness of soul Hannah wept much and prayed to the Lord.
And she made a vow, saying, 'O Lord Almighty, if you will
only look upon your servant's misery and remember me, and
not forget your servant but give her a son, then I will give
him to the Lord for all the days of his life.'*

Yet, even before God answered, Hannah was able to
find peace and contentment, God's gracious comfort in
her distress, because she cast her misery on the Lord by
way of prayer. She fervently poured out her soul to Him
and learned to completely trust God with the outcome.
How many times do we give our worries and sorrows to
the Lord, only to take them right back again? And how

many times do we ask and ask only to receive without ever truly praising and thanking Him? Hannah never forgot to thank God. Her story ends in a prayer of grateful celebration of God's goodness. Hannah's prayer of thanksgiving was not just for the precious gift of Samuel; it was offered to God because He is awesome and powerful, the one and holy God.

Wanderer, Pray

The starry night shall tidings bring:
Go out upon the breezy moor —
Watch for a bird with sable wing,
And beak and talons dropping gore.

Look not around, look not beneath,
But mutely trace its airy way —
Mark where it lights upon the heath;
Then wanderer, kneel thee down and pray.

What fortune may await thee there,
I will not, and I dare not tell;
But heaven is moved by fervent prayer
And God Is mercy; fare thee well!
~ Emily Bronte

Heaven is moved by fervent prayer. Pray to God. Trust Him with your greatest sorrow and pray as Hannah — from your heart, the depths of your soul, with great devotion and submission to His will.

~ Life Application ~

Hannah was praying in her heart, and her lips were moving but her voice was not heard. 1 Samuel 1:12

1. Read 1 Samuel chapters 1 and 2. What did you learn from this story? Perhaps how to pray in faith, or how Hannah kept her promise to God. Be specific.

    _____

    _____

    _____

2. What do John 14:13-14 and Matthew 21:22 say about prayer? Write down one of these verses and claim it for your life.

    _____

    _____

    _____

3. First Samuel 2:1-2 states: *Then Hannah prayed and said: 'My heart rejoices in the Lord; in the Lord my horn is lifted high. My mouth boasts over my enemies, for I delight in your deliverance. There is no one holy like the Lord; There is no one besides you; There is no Rock like our God.* Write out your own prayer of exaltation and thanksgiving — lift high His sovereign name.

    _____

    _____

    _____

~ Journal ~

The name *Samuel* means, "asked of God." Today, think about the "Samuels" of your life. Write them in your journal — then thank and praise God for answering your prayers.

_____

_____

_____

_____

_____

_____

_____

_____

_____

_____

_____

_____

_____

_____

_____

_____

_____

_____

_____

_____

_____

Write It Down

Date Made	Prayer Request	Date Received
————	————————————————	————
————	————————————————	————
————	————————————————	————
————	————————————————	————
————	————————————————	————
————	————————————————	————
————	————————————————	————
————	————————————————	————
————	————————————————	————
————	————————————————	————
————	————————————————	————
————	————————————————	————
————	————————————————	————
————	————————————————	————
————	————————————————	————
————	————————————————	————
————	————————————————	————
————	————————————————	————
————	————————————————	————
————	————————————————	————
————	————————————————	————
————	————————————————	————
————	————————————————	————
————	————————————————	————
————	————————————————	————

Write It Down

Date Made	Prayer Request	Date Received
_____	_____	_____
_____	_____	_____
_____	_____	_____
_____	_____	_____
_____	_____	_____
_____	_____	_____
_____	_____	_____
_____	_____	_____
_____	_____	_____
_____	_____	_____
_____	_____	_____
_____	_____	_____
_____	_____	_____
_____	_____	_____
_____	_____	_____
_____	_____	_____
_____	_____	_____
_____	_____	_____
_____	_____	_____
_____	_____	_____
_____	_____	_____
_____	_____	_____
_____	_____	_____
_____	_____	_____

Endnotes

[1] "The Road Not Taken," from *The Poetry of Robert Frost*

[2] John 11:25 as quoted in *A Tale of Two Cities* by Charles Dickens.

[3] *A Tale of Two Cities* by Charles Dickens.

[4] *Corrie ten Boom* by Sam Wellman.©1997 by Barbour & Company, Uhrichsville, OH. Used by permission.

[5] Psalm 20:4

[6] Excerpt from *All But My Life* by Gerda Weismann Klein. Copyright © 1957 and copyright renewed © 1995 by Gerda Weissmann Klein. Reprinted by permission of Hill and Wang, a division of Farrar, Straus and Giroux, LLC.

Notes

Notes

Notes

Notes

Notes

Notes

Notes

Notes